By the same author

WANTING THE IMPOSSIBLE
MASTERY IN THE STORM
THE LIFE OF CONTINUAL REJOICING
LIVING THE CHRISTIAN LIFE

PASTOR AND PEOPLE

A Devotional Commentary on II Corinthians

GEORGE B. DUNCAN

WORD BOOKS
LONDON

Published by Word Books, London,
a Division of Word (UK) Ltd, Park Lane,
Hemel Hempstead, Hertfordshire.

ISBN 0 85009 037 7

First published June 1972

Made and printed in Great Britain by
Hunt Barnard Printing Ltd., Aylesbury,
Bucks.

FOREWORD

It is a great privilege for me to write the Foreword to this book, whose author is a personal friend whom I esteem highly in the Lord. George Duncan's ministry is always marked by two unique qualities, namely authority and tenderness. I say unique, because it is not often that these things are combined in the ministry of one man.

They have been developed through many years of experience in pulpits of strategic churches in Britain, notably in his present ministry at St. George's-Tron, Glasgow. Only those who have had any experience of leadership in a church located in the centre of a city know the tensions and battles which God has used to endue His servant with such heavenly authority in his preaching, and such Holy Spirit tenderness revealed in his compassion and concern for the individual.

In the publication of this book these qualities have unmistakably been conveyed in the printed page, and therefore I am confident that it will be of immense help to all who are engaged in the Christian ministry at such an hour as this, when the pressures at home and overseas upon all who are in any position of leadership are almost overwhelming. Many will find encouragement, strength, new hope, and vision in the reading of this book, as indeed I have done.

Also, it seems to me that there could be a very valuable and wide use for a book of this nature in one of the most remarkable developments in recent years of Christian outreach in almost every country. I refer to the increase of home Bible study groups. I can visualise a considerable circulation and usefulness for this volume in such situations. The down-to-earth treatment of such subjects as suffering, stewardship, Christian responsibility and service, among others, will be found of the utmost value for group discussion as well as of the greatest blessing in personal experience.

It is therefore with the utmost pleasure that I commend this most recent work of Mr. Duncan's to the wide circle of people who I am sure will find it to be of inestimable value.

Alan Redpath,
June 1972

INTRODUCTION

The following chapters represent notes of Bible Studies given to my own congregation at our mid-week Fellowship of Prayer and Bible Study in St. George's-Tron Church in Glasgow. In these studies I have not attempted a verse by verse exposition of what Paul has written, but rather I have tried to analyse the main thrust of what he has had to say. Verse by verse exposition can already be had in many commentaries, but these studies are designed to find out what the message of St. Paul is, and then to apply it to the local situation. I question if there is any relationship more vital in the life and fellowship of a church than the relationship that exists between the minister and his people. It is this relationship that lies at the heart of this wonderful epistle and I only hope and pray that as a result of these studies that relationship may be strengthened and greatly enriched to the advancement of Christ's Kingdom and the building up of His church.

I owe a great debt to many people, to several commentaries, and my debt to these will be recognised as you read the chapters that follow. I suppose the greatest debt I owe is to those members of my church who, by their attendance and affection and close attention and appreciation, made the giving of these Bible Studies a joy to myself and, I trust, a blessing to them.

In submitting these Bible Studies to the publishers the idea gained ground in our minds that they could serve varying purposes: first of all purely as a book of personal devotion, and an aid to reading the Bible in private but also as a kind of handbook for Bible Study Groups either in homes or in churches or in Christian Unions. My one desire is that the lessons and views that this great apostle has revealed in this letter may come through to our own minds and our own situations and there prove fruitful. It is with the prayer that God's rich blessing may rest upon these studies that I venture to send them forth.

I must add a special word of thanks to Miss Mona Moar, my secretary, through whose diligent work the production of this book has been made possible, and to Miss Margaret Brown for the questions she has added to each chapter with a view to stimulating thought and discussion.

GEORGE B. DUNCAN

CONTENTS

This book is gratefully dedicated to

THE FAITHFUL CHURCH MEMBER

that wonderful person whose praises go so largely unsung, but without whose regular attendance, constant dependability, faithful intercession, lasting affection, unstinted generosity in the giving of time money and strength, the work of the pastor would not be possible

"I thank my God upon every remembrance of you" Phil. 1. 3.

Chapter 1

THE SCHOOL OF SUFFERING

Passage studied II Corinthians 1:1–11

Introduction: This letter was in all probability written from Philippi to Corinth. While it is called in our Bibles the second letter it is obvious from what we read in this epistle that there have been other letters which have no doubt been lost. We can gather this from chapter 2:4 where Paul refers to an earlier letter in such a way as would not make it descriptive of the first epistle. This letter that we are studying was obviously occasioned by the return of Titus. It seems possible that Titus may have taken the missing letter to Corinth and Paul had sent for him to see how things were going after the receipt of that missing letter. It may be that it was severe in its tone and Paul was concerned about the effect it would have. All this can be deduced from chapter 7 vv. 6–9 where the report that Titus brought back indicated that the Corinthians had reacted well. It has been said that this epistle is the most like a letter of all the epistles, revealing all the twists and turns of thought in the mind of the apostle, the changing moods and emotions, the insights and experience of a pastor who is concerned about the spiritual wellbeing of his people. Bishop Handley Moule says 'Where in Holy Scripture do we come closer to this eager and wonderful personality than in this epistle. Reading this epistle we feel as if we can see his face, touch his hand, catch the accent of his voice and detect the tears in his tired eyes.' Bishop Handley Moule calls it 'this glorious oracle of God.' Here then is revealed more fully than anywhere all that is involved in the relationship between a pastor and his people. This by way of introduction. Our first study then is titled:

'The School of Suffering'

Rather unusually Paul begins, after his customary greetings, with himself. In most of his epistles he moves into thanksgiving, after greeting his readers; thanksgiving for God's goodness to those and in those to whom he writes. The Church at Corinth possibly had given him so much cause for concern that he begins differently. He begins with himself and strangely enough with his sufferings and the grace of God that had sustained him. In this approach it has been suggested that there is a tacit appeal to the sympathy of his readers and hearers. The Corinthians had shown themselves hostile to Paul and in a rare moment of self-revelation encouraged by the good report of Titus, Paul lets them see something of the burden and wounds, the existence of which in all probability they had no inkling. A pastor, he suggests, knows much of suffering without those who owed so much to him under God adding to it. Four gleams of light shine out from the dark clouds of this opening section:

A. THE INTENSITY EXPOSED

I wonder if his hearers listened with a sense of shock as Paul's opening sentences were read. What a different man he was from what they had imagined him to be. So often the picture we make of personalities is quite unrelated to the hard facts. Paul tells them how he had found out that to be in the service of Christ was to receive the same kind of treatment as Christ received. And so in v.5 he speaks of 'the sufferings of Christ' as abounding in him. In v.9 in J. B. Phillips translation he speaks of 'coming to the end of our tether'. First of all let us note:

(a) *The nature of his sufferings* He calls them the sufferings of Christ – that is to say there are certain sufferings that come our way in the service of Jesus Christ just as they came Christ's way. These are sufferings that come to us because we are Christians. Christians share the very life of Christ, they live the same way, they are concerned about the same things, they suffer in the same way. The suffering of Christ in which we share came to Him along two lines and it will come to us along the same two lines. First of all in His treatment at the hands of men in the rejection of His message and also in His acceptance of the will of God in the redemption He achieved for others. His acceptance of the will of God meant getting under the burden of the world's sin. This is not a thought strange to the mind of Paul – in Colossians 1:24 he speaks of 'filling up that which is lacking of the affliction of Christ' and in Hebrews 13:13 the writer speaks about going without the camp 'bearing his reproach'. We need to remember that the badge of Christian service is not a cushion but a cross. Professor William Barclay quotes Samuel Rutherford as writing to one of his friends and saying 'God has called you to Christ's side and the wind is now in Christ's face in this land, and seeing you are with Him you cannot expect the lee-side or the sunny side of the brae'.

(b) *The measure of his sufferings* v.8b 'we were pressed out of measure, above strength, insomuch that we despaired even of life itself' The R.S.V. translates 'we were so utterly and unbearably crushed that we despaired of life itself' J. B. Phillips 'we were completely overwhelmed, the burden was more than we could bear in fact we told ourselves that this was the end'. Later on in the epistle Paul sets out a catalogue of suffering and pain which he ends by saying 'and beside those things which are without that which cometh upon me daily the care of all the churches' Paul was a man burdened and bruised like his Lord and like every other true servant of Christ. To this burden and to these bruises, of the very existence of which in their ignorance they knew nothing, they had added by their actions and by their words. The exact experience to which Paul is referring in v.8 is not known. It may have been an accumulation of suffering which had gathered and to which some final addition had come, that suddenly made the whole weight unsupportable. Paul found himself 'at the end of his tether'. How often it is this accumulation of pain that suddenly makes even a tiny intensification of it unbearable. How carefully we ought to regard one another lest in even a small or slight word of comment or criticism we add the final straw that 'breaks the camel's back'. But it is important to note that all this is revealed factually not with any trace of self pity. As someone has said 'what are soldiers for but to be shot at'. He speaks also here of:

B. THE ADEQUACY EXPERIENCED

The word most frequently found in these verses is the word comfort derived from a Latin word meaning strong or brave. The word comes nine times in five verses. Bishop Handley Moule translates it by the word 'encouragement' but I wonder if that is sufficiently communicative. If the result of my being strengthened is that I am encouraged then the translation is all right. Paul refers to this adequacy as being experienced for two reasons:

(a) *The power by which he had been strengthened* v.4 'God who comforteth us in all our tribulation, the comfort wherewith we ourselves are comforted of God'. v.10 'Who delivered us, and doth deliver, and will yet deliver'. v.5 'through Christ we share abundantly in comfort.' In that very situation which had brought him to despair even of life itself there had come an experience of a greater strength, a greater courage than his own. The whole testimony of Christian experience is to the effect that God does not necessarily take us out of a situation but He gives us strength to win through. I remember hearing of a prayer offered by somebody who said, 'Lord either lighten the load or strengthen my back' and it is usually the strengthening of our backs that is the answer that God gives to our prayer. Do you remember how in writing to the Romans in Romans 8:37 Paul says 'in all these things we are more than conquerors through him that loved us' I remember being so challenged by the first two words 'in all'. In a sermon preached at Keswick some years ago and printed in my book 'Wanting The Impossible' I suggest that these two words cover the sphere of our victory. And taking each word in turn they speak of first of all, that sphere from which *no escape is provided* – 'in all these things' – not away from them but *in* them: and also that sphere of life from which *no exception is permitted* – in all – not in some but in all these things we are more than conquerors. But Paul also refers to:

(b) *The prayers by which he had been sustained* v.11 'ye also helping together by prayer for us' What a lot Paul owed to the prayers of others, and here he is gracious and generous enough to believe that even in the Church at Corinth where so many people had been so unkind and so unfriendly to him there had been those none the less who had prayed for him and would still go on praying for him. We can never estimate how much our prayers achieve – only eternity will reveal. It is encouraging to note that this is something we can all do for those engaged in the service of God. We do not all have the money to give, we do not all have the strength to work, we do not all have the ability to serve, but we all have the time to pray and we all as born again Christians have the right to pray. No wonder Paul handles his sufferings with a song. The third gleam of light that shines from the dark clouds of suffering is that Paul had found:

C. THE MINISTRY, ENRICHED

In writing out all that he had experienced, all that he had endured, Paul could see two things of immense value:

(a) *A greater usefulness in his ministry* v.4 'that we may be able to comfort those which are in any trouble' His usefulness had been increased in two ways. First of all there would be *the sympathy that he would now have with those who were suffering* and also there would be *the testimony he could now bear.* Having experienced God's sustaining grace, he could with confidence tell others that they too would experience God's sustaining grace. What a difference it makes if we understand, and people sense that we understand, and if we know that God has the answer. This brought a greater usefulness unquestionably in his ministry – Paul had no doubt about this. And so all through his suffering he was conscious of the fact that there was a purpose to be served which lay beyond himself and beyond his sufferings that touched other lives. Professor William Barclay quotes Barrie as saying about his own mother who lost her favourite son 'that is where my mother got her soft eyes and why other mothers come to her when they have lost a child'. What a difference it makes when we say 'I have been there, I know what you are going through and I know just how God's grace sustains!' So Paul could see a positive gain in his ministry through his sufferings. Do you recall how it was said of Christ Himself in Hebrews 4:15 'We have not an high priest which cannot be touched with the feeling of our infirmities, but was in all points tempted like as we are, yet without sin. Let us therefore come boldly unto the throne of grace that we may obtain mercy and find grace to help in time of need.' We come there and we come to Him because we know He understands. A greater usefulness, and paradoxically enough:

(b) *A greater helplessness in his ministry* One of the results, one of the effects of his intense suffering he reveals in v.9 'that we should not trust in ourselves but in God' The greatest menace in Christian service is a sense of self sufficiency. The basic principle of all Christian usefulness was laid down by our Lord Himself 'without me ye can do nothing'. The constant peril is to forget this and the kind of experience that Paul had gone through had proved a salutary one – his own resources had been exhausted and he had been thrown back utterly upon God. Recently there was sent to me a book with a very suggestive title. It was titled 'Crowded to Christ'. How easy to forget our helplessness, how easy to be busy in God's work without relying upon Him, to stop praying, to neglect the person and ministry of the Holy Spirit. And there in the school of suffering we discover ourselves again to be weak and poor and foolish – and so we turn to Him.

THE INTENSITY EXPOSED: THE ADEQUACY EXPERIENCED: THE MINISTRY ENRICHED and finally:

D. THE DISCOVERIES ENJOYED

To discover something new is always a delight whether it be a new recipe or a new friend. Paul had made two discoveries through the suffering that had come his way. First of all:

(a) *He discovered a new name for his Lord* 'the Father of all mercies, the God of all comfort' In these new circumstances he had discovered new facets in the character and grace of his God. Professor James Denny quotes concerning this name it is 'a name wonderful in its tenderness'. So often this is true of life. We have friends, we think we know them well and then suddenly we find ourselves in touch with them in an entirely new set of circumstances and we see them in an entirely new light; and our comment may be in their favour or may be not – our comment has been 'I did not know she was that kind of person' I wonder if this was Paul's comment concerning his Lord 'I did not know that He was that kind of God – the God of all comfort'. The second discovery enjoyed by Paul was:

(b) *He discovered a new song in his Heart.* This whole section opens in v.3 with the word 'blessed'. The N.E.B.

translates it 'praise' Handley Moule translates it 'praised with worshipping love'. And so, as I mentioned earlier, there is no trace of self pity in this description of the school of suffering but rather the spirit of praise and thanksgiving and worshipping love. This ties in with the words of James who you remember said to the tried and suffering Christians to whom he wrote 'count it all joy when you fall into different trials' Paul starts the song but he knows that others will share it; for this section ends in v.11 with the reminder not only that many have prayed for him but that as their prayers were answered so they would join together in giving thanks and praising God. So although Paul starts the song others share it. One translation ends this section with these words 'that there may be a sea of upturned faces as a widespread thanksgiving goes up to God on our behalf for the gracious act which He has done for us'. I remember reading of a Jew who had been driven out of Germany through the persecution of the Jews under the Nazi regime: he had lost his all but he had found his Lord and his comment was significant 'It is better that we arrive beaten and bleeding at a glorious goal than that we decay happily and contented in darkness'. Paul realised that he had passed through the school of suffering but that he had reached a glorious goal although beaten and bleeding yet rejoicing.

Let us remember then that if we commit ourselves to the service of Christ we commit ourselves to His sufferings, but at the same time let us be careful lest we who are Christians add to the sufferings of the servants of God needlessly and make their suffering unbearable.

QUESTIONS FOR DISCUSSION

Study No. 1 – II Corinthians 1:1–11

1. 'Do not expect the Christian life to be a bed of roses!'

From this passage, how might we back up this warning to young Christians? What fresh light is thrown upon the character of God, when we find ourselves suffering?

2. 'I thought Paul would not be subject to trials.'

   Are any Christians without trials? In what way can they be 'above' them?

3. The three most commonly mentioned ideas in this section are – 'trials, comfort, thanksgiving'.

   What is the relationship between the Christian and his God in each of these? What should be the inter-relationship of pastor and people in each?

Chapter 2

PAUL AND HIS CRITICS

Passage studied II Corinthians 1:12–2:11

In our second study of Paul's letter to the Christian Church in Corinth we find Paul dealing with his critics, and it is worth noting that he was the object of criticism, and if such an outstanding Christian was criticized by other Christians then we may well expect to be criticized ourselves. So let us not be surprised or dismayed if people do have unkind things to say about us. What we want to do is to see here how Paul reacted to criticism and how he handled it: how he had been misrepresented by those who sought to denigrate his character. As we look at this section where Paul is replying to his critics we find three things emerging from the experience through which he had passed:

A. THE STANDARD HE SETS IN HIS SERVICE

Paul was in trouble at Corinth, at least he had been, and one of the factors that had given cause for criticism and complaint had been a change in plan that he had made. Instead of going to Macedonia through Corinth and returning back to Asia Minor through Corinth he had decided on one visit only and now he would travel from Asia Minor to Corinth via Macedonia. Paul refers to his original plans in v.16 of chapter 1, and to the change of plans in v.23 of chapter 1. It is worth noting:
(a) *The ignorance behind the criticism* In v.14 Paul lays his finger on the weakness of the position of his critics. The N.E.B. translates that verse 'partial as your present knowledge is of us'. The trouble behind so much criticism

is ignorance: our knowledge as critics or the knowledge of our critics is only partial. The fact is that we just don't know enough about any situation to make a fair judgment or fair assessment – that happens far more often than we think. This is all brought out especially clearly in v.23 of chapter 1 when Paul is explaining why he had changed his plans. They had made their own deductions from the change of plans. Paul, they said, was completely unreliable. He said 'yes' and all the time he meant 'no'. But if only they had known the real motivation behind the change of plans, that it was 'out of consideration' for them, it was 'to spare you', they would have reached a very different conclusion. This is of course the basic weakness of so much criticism – not necessarily of all – but of a great deal. The truth is we just don't know enough, and I am afraid that very often the trouble is that we don't even want to know. All we want is an excuse, something to justify our criticism. We love criticizing other people especially those whose standard of life is in itself a rebuke of our own. It is quite obvious that the spirit of suspicion and mistrust had spread so that there were those who were even querying the sincerity and truth of what he had written in his letters to them. If a man was unreliable in his deeds how were they to know that he was not equally unreliable in his words. And so the spirit of criticism can grow until the whole of a man's influence for God is undermined. Paul is hinting at these suspicious doubts in chapter 1:13 where J. B. Phillips translates 'our letters to you have no double meaning – they mean just what you understand them to mean when you read them'. It was of course an extremely serious situation in the mind of Paul when they were doubting his message. And so we see the ignorance behind the criticism and we also see:

(b) *The confidence before the criticism* Paul lifts the lid a little bit. He draws back the curtain of that reserve which is so right and proper in God's servant engaged in God's service. Just as a doctor will not always explain what he is doing – it would take too much time – so those who are in God's service do not always necessarily explain what they are doing because again it would take too much time. But Paul apparently feels the situation is serious enough to warrant a reply. He is concerned about the damage to the whole Church that could result if he did not speak. And this concern for the wellbeing of the Church makes him speak thankfully and confidently. Who was it who said 'my strength is as the strength of ten because my heart is pure'. Paul's conscience is absolutely clear. He was not moved in any decision he made concerning his work by earthly wisdom but by divine grace. This is what he is referring to in v.12. My conscience, he says, is absolutely clear on that point. The N.E.B. translates v.12 'our conduct has been governed by a devout and godly sincerity'. The R.S.V. translates 'holiness and godly sincerity'. And that word sincerity means a perfect openness towards God. Paul sought to live and serve his Lord in a way that was always exposed to the judgment and evaluation of God Himself. And a life that is lived there is not upset by the judgments of men. This is possibly one reason why a Christian engaged in the Lord's service is not generally so easily upset by criticism as a non-Christian. Paul brings this out in his first letter to the Corinthian Church – I Corinthians 4:3 'with me it is a very small thing that I should be judged of you, or of man's judgment: I do not even judge myself. He that judgeth me is the Lord'. It was Charles Spurgeon who said 'You can take the story of my life and write it across the sky. I have nothing to hide'. It is because of this openness towards God that Paul shows his confidence towards his critics. And if you and I have a clear conscience that, as best as we know how, we are doing what God wants us to do in the way that He wants us to do it and that we are not double-minded or insincere or moved by other or lesser motives, we can be quite confident as we face our critics. But Paul could not have shown this confidence if he had not set this standard in his work. And so the first thing that we see as Paul faces his critics is THE STANDARD HE SETS IN HIS WORK FOR HIS LORD. Secondly we see:

B. THE SAVIOUR HE SERVED IN HIS WORK

Paul was acutely aware of the fact that anything said against the servant could become something said against the Saviour. And so we see two lines of thought emerging after he has spoken of the standard that he sets in his work. Paul is concerned first of all about:

(a) *The Name that might be clouded.* If the servant was fickle and unreliable, if his words were not trustworthy, if his actions were unpredictable, what kind of a Saviour did that servant have? Paul replies that fickleness in a servant of Jesus Christ was quite unthinkable. It would be totally unbecoming in the servant of a Saviour of Whose faithfulness there could be no doubt at all. God fickle! God's word untrustworthy! Perish the thought. There is a valid point however here to which we would do well to pay heed. Whether we like it or not the opinion people have of Christians has a very close link with the opinion people have of Christ. How often the attitude they adopt is expressed in the phrase 'If that is what it means to be a Christian then I don't want to have anything to do with the Church'. Of course it is quite unfair, it is quite unreasonable but nevertheless people are unfair, they are unreasonable, and our job is to see that we give them no grounds for drawing such a conclusion. We need to remember that people are not likely to trust our Saviour if they cannot trust us. This is the line along which Paul's argument is developing in vv.17–20. He is concerned about the Name of his faithful Lord that might be clouded by a charge of unfaithfulness in that Lord's servant. And so we see secondly that Paul is anxious about:

(b) *The Name that must be cleared.* Paul seeks to clear the Name of Christ first of all by giving a full explanation of his action to refute their charge of fickleness, and then by stressing the fact that fickleness could never be characteristic of a life in which the Spirit of the living and faithful God has come to dwell. In v.15 he tells them that the original plans had been based upon the existence of a mutual confidence between himself and the Corinthian Church. Subsequent events and reports indicated that confidence had been destroyed in the minds of many of the Corinthian Christians, and because the confidence had been destroyed the plans had then been changed. In v.23 following he points out that had he come he would have had to have rebuked them but he did not want to do this so he had changed his plans to spare them, and to spare himself the unpleasantness that might have resulted from their meeting in these circumstances. It was not fickleness in him but tenderness for them that had decided his line of action. He wanted to help them spiritually but this could only happen in an atmosphere of mutual confidence. It would have been a waste of time, it would have been worse than a waste of time to have come under any other circumstances. Having therefore given an explanation to refute their charge of fickleness he then moves on to assert that there was no dubiety about the message he had preached – Jesus Christ was God's emphatic 'yes' and 'Amen' to every promise of grace in the Old Testament. And it was the Spirit, the Holy Spirit of this God, this faithful God that indwelt the servants of this God, and this made them as faithful as He was. Faithfulness and reliability in a Christian constitute part of the evidence of the presence and ministry of the Holy Spirit in his life.

THE STANDARD HE SET: THE SAVIOUR HE SERVED: and then we see thirdly:

C. THE SORROW HE SHUNNED IN HIS WORK

Chapter 2:1 'I determined this that I would not come again to you in heaviness.' Paul was very deeply concerned about two things. First:

(a) *The sadness that must cease.* Sadness was not in keeping with the Gospel which is a gospel of joy. The sadness had been twofold. It had been due to *the disturbance and disruption of their fellowship.* Paul had been saddened by the action he had had to take. In v.4 of chapter 2 he refers to an earlier letter, which is sometimes called 'the painful letter', that he had written 'out of much affliction and anguish of heart I wrote unto you with many tears'. It was out of the sadness of a heart that had been hurt by what had been done to it and by what it had had to do to others to remedy the situation. This letter of rebuke he had had to write but it had given him no pleasure and he wanted this unhappiness to cease. He wanted the relationship of confidence and joy to be restored. But the sadness had also been caused by *the discipline applied to the offender.* Apparently one man had been at the root of all the trouble. He is referred to in v.5 and the verses that follow. He had been disciplined in order that the offence that he had caused should cease. But Paul was distressed by it all and was concerned lest this man, through the discipline administered to him should be driven to despair. There is nothing so saddening in the fellowship of the Christian Church as the trouble that one person can so often cause. It happens again, and again, and again. And where there is this disharmony, where there is this hurtful comment, this continual narking and nagging, the joy and the happiness of the fellowship is bound to suffer. Paul longed that the sadness should cease. And so we see also in the mind of Paul here:

(b) *The gladness that must come* to the whole fellowship. This is brought out in chapter 2:2 – 'If I cause you pain, who is there to make me glad' and in v.3 'I wrote as I did so that I might not be pained by those who should have made me rejoice'. The mutual relationship between pastor and people should be one of mutual happiness. Each finds joy and happiness in the other. We are not quite certain what had motivated the criticism of Paul that had hurt so deeply and that had called for his reply. If we think in terms of the background of the Corinthian Christian Church, a pagan licentious city, so loose in its living that the proverb was well known 'to live like a Corinthian' – as being synonymous of a completely immoral life, it is possible that part of the grudge against Paul took the line that he was a killjoy. The way of life set out in Christ seemed to have no room for so much that the average Corinthian deemed essential for happiness. Paul was making the way difficult, and narrow, and demanding. Compared with the seeming freedom and gaiety of the average Corinthian the way Paul set out seemed drab and colourless. We know of course that the Christian life is not a joyless life. It never was so in the mind of Christ nor was it so in the mind of Paul. The difference between the Christian way of joy and that of the world is that the Christian way of joy leads to joy. The worldling's way of joy leads to disillusionment. And so although this experience of Paul among his critics was disturbed and darkened by suspicion and doubts, yet in all his speaking here we get glimpses and glints of light, and sunshine, and joy, which Paul makes quite clear are what he is seeking for them and that their joy is his joy. And so v.3 he writes 'that my joy would be the joy of you'. To the one man who has caused the trouble he asks a display of love, a restraint in discipline, so that he may be forgiven and restored. And with the fellowship restored and complete the enemy of souls would be defeated, for underlying all this ferment, all this hurtful talk Paul sensed the activity of the enemy of souls. This is a sobering thought. The enemy of souls is called 'the accuser of the brethren' and we need to be very careful when we open our mouths in comment that is critical and unkind and sometimes untrue of others, we need to be very careful lest we find ourselves doing the Devil's own work. If we become the accusers of the brethren let us make no mistake about it we are taking sides with the Devil for that is his work, that's the work that he loves to do. And if he can get some of us who name the name of Christ to do it all the better for him. You say that that is unthinkable that a Christian should be the mouthpiece of the Devil but is it really unthinkable? Do you remember the words our Lord spoke to Peter after his great confession in reply to the question – Whom say ye that I am? And Peter replied, 'Thou art the Christ, the Son of the living God'. In a few moments after that the Lord was speaking of His death at Calvary and Peter immediately took it upon himself to rebuke his Master, 'far be it from Thee' only to merit and receive the stern rebuke from the lips of Christ 'Get thee behind Me, Satan'. So if Peter can be the mouthpiece of Satan so can you, and so can I.

QUESTIONS FOR DISCUSSION

Study No. 2 – II Corinthians 1:12–2:11

1. By what standard is our sincerity measured? How should this affect our words and actions?
2. Paul knew himself to be the object of criticism at this time. What was his attitude, and what should be ours, to criticism of and by our fellow Christians?
3. For what reasons, with what motive, and to what extent may a pastor rebuke his people? or What factors may govern a pastor in rebuking his people?
4. What should be the Christian's chief concern – others' opinion of himself or of Christ?

Chapter 3

PAUL'S CONCEPTION OF HIS MINISTRY

Passage studied II Corinthians 2:12–3:3

In beginning these studies in Paul's second letter to the Corinthians we made the point that in this letter we come to understand more of the mind and moods of St. Paul, his feelings and his emotions than in any other epistle, and that in this epistle a great deal is revealed concerning the relationship between a Pastor and his People. In this section Paul allows the Christians at Corinth to get some idea of what his responsibilities in Christian service and ministry meant to Paul. They had had their ideas: and in the last study, when we were dealing with Paul and his critics, Paul had pointed out to them the peril of partial knowledge. Now he would give them fuller knowledge still – fuller insight. So often we do not see things from the point of view of other people. When we do it opens our eyes to a whole area of thought and truth about which previously we had been totally ignorant. The ministry and Christian service for Paul held first of all:

A. THE OPPORTUNITIES THAT MUST BE SEIZED

In vv.12 and 13 he speaks of the way in which 'a door was opened' when he came to Troas. He had travelled north on his way to Macedonia and suddenly found an opportunity to preach the gospel at Troas. There are two thoughts that come to mind as I read these two verses. First of all:

(a) *Where the opportunity could lead.* When he speaks of the opening of a door surely this suggests that the door was a door to be entered, to be passed through. And what discoveries would be made when the door had been entered – discoveries of people to be blessed of whose very existence he had until then been quite unaware, and through these people of places to be influenced for God through the gospel. In Revelation 3:8 Christ speaks to the Church at Philadelphia, saying, 'I have set before thee an open door, and no man can shut it' This is one of the exciting things about being available for Christian service, not necessarily, and not only, in the specialised sense in which Paul was available but in the sense in which every Christian ought to be available, for we will continually be finding that doors of opportunity are open. All that God asks is our obedience, an obedience that will act and an obedience that will lead on into the most surprising experiences of people and places. People to be reached with the gospel. This can happen in an office, in a hospital, in a shop, in a factory – anywhere. Suddenly we find a door opened. Somebody speaks to us. We discover somebody in trouble. And the opportunity is there right ahead, and behind that person may be a home, behind that person may be a Church, a Bible Class. Who knows! So for Paul being in the ministry and being in Christian service meant opportunities that must be seized and he was excited at the thought of where the opportunities could lead. But in these verses we see also: (b) *Why the opportunity was lost* for it was lost. J. B. Phillips translates v.13 'I was on edge the whole time because there was no sign of Titus. So I said goodbye and went from them to Macedonia.' The opportunity in Troas was lost because of the situation at Corinth. Paul was waiting for news from Titus on his return and no news had come, and Paul was so concerned about a Church at Corinth that he couldn't settle to the work in Troas. How solemn and serious a warning this verse holds, and the warning is simply this – that Christians who cause trouble can absorb time and strength that should be given in Christian outreach to others. James Denny comments thus 'If the Corinthians were capable of reflection they might reflect with shame on the loss which their sin had entailed on the people of Troas' and then he adds 'They could not but feel how genuine was the apostle's love when he had made such a sacrifice to it. But such a sacrifice ought never to have been required.' Oh, the waste of time and effort and energy, and opportunity because difficult Christians absorb the spiritual effort and energy that could and should have been directed towards other people. Apparently in Corinth, at the heart of the problem, was one man and it is quite amazing how much trouble one or two people can cause in the fellowship of a Church. We want to pray that we may never be the cause of this kind of confusion and this kind of impoverishment of the total impact of the witness of the Church of Jesus Christ. We are not of course dealing here with young Christians who need to be nurtured or Christians who have fallen and need to be helped: we are dealing with Christians who are deliberately causing trouble and hindering the work of the gospel. And so for Paul being in Christian service and in the Christian ministry was a thrilling experience. It held for him *the opportunity that must be seized.* What else did the ministry hold for Paul? Well, it spoke to him also of:

B. A VICTORY THAT WOULD BE SHARED

It may have been Paul's recollection of the thrill that filled his heart when Titus did meet him at Philippi that led him off into the shout of triumph that follows. Two aspects of the following verses must be kept in mind:
(a) *The illustration we find here.* The illustration upon which Paul is drawing is that of the triumph of a victorious Roman general. And that is Paul's conception of Christian service. Christ has triumphed and does triumph and we are asked to share in that triumph. The R.S.V. translates v.14 as follows 'Thanks be to God who in Christ always leads us in triumph, and through us spreads

the fragrance of the knowledge of Him everywhere'. The question is – how does He lead us? Is it as His prisoner? It does not specifically say so, although this is the interpretation that Denney puts upon it. Denney makes a perfectly valid theological point, namely, that it is not until we have submitted to Christ that we share in His triumph. It could be that He leads us as His soldiers, marching behind Him, following His lead, rejoicing in His victory. It could be as the sharers of His life. It could be literally as the R.S.V. renders it 'Thanks be to God who in Christ always leads us in triumph' that is to say, God sees us literally in Christ – part of Him – the victor. There is a chorus that we used to sing with great fervour in our young days. 'On the victory side, On the victory side, No foe can daunt me, No fear can haunt me, On the victory side. On the victory side, On the victory side, With Christ within The fight we'll win, On the victory side.' Part of the procession of a triumph would be made up of priests and they would no doubt be carrying incense. And as the procession moved through the cheering crowds the perfume and fragrance of this incense would spread everywhere. This lies behind the words of Paul 'through us He spreads the fragrance of the knowledge of Him everywhere'. It is meant to be so with the Christian. There should be a fragrance, an attractive graciousness about a Christian's life, about the way he behaves, about the way he speaks that would compel attention. Sometimes it may be you have passed a garden in which there has been growing some night-scented stock. This flower sheds its perfume and fragrance only at night. I have known the experience quite frequently of suddenly stopping as I have been passing a garden and saying, 'where's that perfume coming from'. There ought to be something arrestingly different about a Christian – a fragrance, an attractiveness that compels attention. This is the illustration we find here. But also as we think of the victory that would be shared there are:

(b) *The implications we face here.* The very scent of the incense that brought smiles and laughter to the faces of the conquerors would speak of defeat and death to the vanquished. It is this thought that makes me question Denney's interpretation of the fact that we are led as His prisoners. We need to remember that the Cross always divides. It did when it was raised and it does when it is preached. The seriousness of the issues raised poses immediately the question 'Who is sufficient for these things?' v.16. And Paul recognises the subtlety of the danger that emerges. The danger of qualifying the message, of corrupting it as the A.V. translates it. Denney tells us that the word used here is the word used of tavern keepers to cover the various devices they would use to deceive their customers and line their own pockets. It can happen to anybody engaged in Christian service. The temptation to avoid the elements in the gospel that would make us unpopular. It can happen in the life of a minister going to a certain Church or wanting to go to a certain Church and discovering that if he is going to be acceptable with the influential members of the congregation he must water down his message and leave out elements that would repel. What we need to remember is that Christ's victory means others defeat, and those who deliberately align themselves with Satan or with error are condemned by the message of the Cross. This is something we dare not shirk. This is a message we dare not corrupt. Let us remember then that when we walk in the triumph of Christ our very witness involves the condemnation of others.

The ministry held for Paul finally:

C. A TESTIMONY THAT COULD BE STUDIED

We have thought of *the opportunity that must be seized* and *the victory that would be shared* and now *the testimony that could be studied.* The final words of v.17 and the reference to the possibility of not presenting the gospel aright sets Paul's mind off on another line of thought. After testifying to the fact that he himself was not guilty of corrupting the Word of God but of preaching it with sincerity Paul would seem to have had in his mind the possibility, or indeed the likelihood, that the very people causing the trouble in Corinth were of the kind that did corrupt the Word of God. They had come with written testimonials but they had obviously tried to undermine Paul's authority. Paul asks the question. Did he need some kind of written authentication of his apostleship. To speak in one's own defence in the face of bitter criticism is not a pleasant experience; it is humiliating to be the subject of it: it is painful to be silent under it; it is degrading to have to speak about it. But Paul feels that the welfare of the Church comes above his own feelings. And so he speaks of the fact that Christian service is rather like the writing of a letter, and the quality of the man can be judged by the contents of the letter. That is to say, the validity of his ministry is judged by the quality of his work. And so Paul speaks of:

(a) *The success that had crowned his work*. 'You' he says, 'are our letter of recommendation' 'You are a letter from Christ'. The changed lives of the Christians at Corinth was the real evidence of the validity and authority of his ministry. He speaks of the Christians there as 'our letter' Christ's letter. The lives lived by the Christian should be the letter read by the world that looked on, and from what they saw in their lives they would form their opinion both of Christ and of Paul His servant. And so he appeals to their own changed lives: he recalls to them the way in which they turned to Christ and the transformation that this meant. This is a sobering thought for any minister, for anybody engaged in Christian service, that the final evaluation of his work is the true success of his ministry, that every congregation is in a sense a reflection of the man. No minister can expect a congregation to rise higher than his own level of spiritual life and devotion. We cannot lead people and expect them to go beyond us, as far as we lead them so they will go. And the judge of any man's ministry is the quality of the Christian's life that is built up under that ministry. And Paul is quite unashamed in appealing to the success, under God, that had marked his visit to Corinth. But he qualifies the success that had crowned his work by acknowledging:

(b) *The Spirit that had done the work* He is under no illusion: he knows that the work was not done by Paul, and so in v.3 he says that the letter was written 'not with ink but with the Spirit of the living God'. Very frequently I am asked for a reference by somebody. I am always happy if it is a reference that I can write happily and confidently, knowing that the person is worthy of the highest commendation and praise. When that letter of reference is presented to the reader for whom it is intended it carries weight in any judgment reached. What Paul is getting at here finally, is that every Christian and every Christian Church is in a sense a reference for Christ. What a sobering thought this is. What kind of a reference is the letter of your life: what kind of a reference is the letter of the life of your church? People will judge Christ, people will judge His servant by what they find in the lives of those influenced by Him. What then is the final test of a ministry? The quality of the spiritual life of the congregation a minister leaves behind. Sobering thought, and one which indicates the tremendous responsibility that rests upon those who are involved in Christian service.

AN OPPORTUNITY TO BE SEIZED, A VICTORY TO BE SHARED, A TESTIMONY TO BE STUDIED. This is Paul's conception of the ministry.

QUESTIONS FOR DISCUSSION

Study No. 3 – II Corinthians 2:12–3:3

1. Consider the implications for the Corinthian Church, for

those at Troas, and for Paul, of his experience at Troas.
What do we, as people or as pastor, learn from this?

2. What should be the governing factor in our proclamation of the Gospel?
3. In what areas of word and work may 'the sweet savour of Christ' be released?
4. There is a poem which concludes:

   'You are writing each day a letter to men –
   Take care that writing is true;
   For the only Gospel that some men will read
   Is the Gospel according to You.'

   Consider this from the point of view of the Pastor, the ordinary Christian, and the man in the street.

Chapter 4

PAUL CONFIDENT ABOUT HIS MESSAGE

Passage studied II Corinthians 3:4–4:6

So far in this epistle we might get the impression that if anything Paul has been on the defensive, giving explanations and seeking understanding from the Christians at Corinth who would seem to have been misled and misguided concerning his attitude towards them and his concern about them. But in this section we find Paul beginning to act and speak more positively, and so we find such phrases as the following: In chapter 3:4 'such is the confidence that we have through Christ toward God' chapter 3:12 'since we have such a hope we are very bold' chapter 4:1 'therefore having this ministry by the mercy of God we do not lose heart'. There comes the time, and there comes the point, when the Christian has to move into the attack. There is a saying in warfare that the best form of defence is attack, and Paul begins now to give positive reasons for his position and states creative truths to correct and counteract the false views that had been put forward by others. And in doing so he is seeking to assure his friends and to answer his foes. From the whole atmosphere of this section which is not too easy to understand it is possible to deduce that part of the trouble at Corinth would seem to have come from Jews who were not prepared to forego so much of the traditions and the truths in which they had been reared and to which they wanted to cling. This was of course a familiar problem everywhere for the Christian Church had been nurtured in the Jewish faith and was finding it difficult, in some ways, to cast off old forms which were now no longer relevant, things which, if insisted on, could prove a hindrance not only to those seeking to enter into the Christian faith but also a hindrance to those who were already within the Church. The kind of question for instance that had already cropped up was – If somebody became a Christian did he need to be circumcised? This, of course, is not a problem confined simply to those coming into the Christian Church from the Jewish faith but to all people coming into the Christian Church. They bring with them naturally traditions and standards, practices and habits, traditions valued by them and precious to them from their previous life. How much of this can they afford to keep? How much of it has to be discarded? But it is of course the particular problem with regard to the relationship between the Jewish practices and the Christian Church that is in the mind of Paul. So our study here falls into three sections. First of all we see:

A. THE EXCELLENCE OF THE PAST SEEN BY PAUL

It is significant and strategically wise that Paul begins by using words of appreciation revealing his understanding of the position of those who obviously were clinging very much to the past. And so he speaks of the glory, or in the R.S.V. the splendour to be found in the Old Covenant. There are two aspects of the past that Paul notes:

(a) *Its worth* and the worth of the Old Covenant surely resided in the fact that in it, and through it, was revealed the moral character of God in His holiness and majesty. The glory of the Old Covenant was essentially its ethical content, its high standard. So often in a temple of some other kind of religion at the very centre of the shrine you would find an image – I remember well visiting the temple of the goddess Kali in Calcutta and peering into the gloom of the innermost sanctuary I saw there the hideous face of this idol. In the Old Testament dispensation and in the Jewish faith both in the Tabernacle and in the Temple in the innermost sanctuary one found the Ten

Commandments – the moral law – in its completeness, in its comprehensiveness, in its challenge. But Paul points out that in itself while this was a glorious and a wonderful and a splendid thing about the Old Covenant it could only lead to despair in the hearts of men striving to keep the commandments: or as so many had found in the light of the Christian revelation it could lead them on to see in Christ the one who had met the requirements of the law on their behalf. And so we find Paul in his epistles stressing this aspect of the Old Covenant. Galatians 3:24 'the law was our schoolmaster to bring us to Christ' Romans 3:20 'by the law is the knowledge of sin'. The glory and splendour of God's holiness and righteousness which lay at the heart of the Old Covenant shone out in all its glory but it shamed in contrast the efforts of men to achieve its standards. And so Paul in this opening section is dealing not only with the worth of the Old Covenant but also:

(b) *Its weakness.* And so we read in v.6 'the written code kills' in v.7 he speaks of 'the dispensation of death' and in v.9 he speaks of 'the dispensation of condemnation'. An ethic can only condemn those who fail to reach its requirements and this was all that the Old Dispensation could do. The glory, the splendour, was there but it offered no hope, it simply brought condemnation and judgment. And so in this section Paul goes on to speak of:

B. THE RELEVANCE OF THE TRUTH PREACHED BY HIM

Just as the brilliance of the street lamps pales before the light of the rising sun so the splendour of the Old Covenant which rested upon man's obedience to the law pales into insignificance before the New Covenant which rests upon man's acceptance of a new life which enables him to keep the law. The glory on the face of Moses faded as time went on, and Paul sees in this an illustration of the fact that the glory of the Old Covenant also faded.

The relevance of the truth preached by him is seen by Paul to be twofold. He speaks of:

(a) *The liberating experience of the New Covenant* chapter 3:17 'where the Spirit of the Lord is there is liberty' And behind the gift of the Holy Spirit Paul of course has in mind all that had preceded His coming, in the incarnation, crucifixion, resurrection and ascension of Jesus Christ. The gift of the Holy Spirit was the climax which crowned everything that Christ had done for men. Paul sees man to be liberated first of all from the demands of the broken law in and through the sacrifice of Christ upon the Cross. But he also sees man to be liberated from the defeat that was constantly his experience as he faced the demands of the law which he found he neither wanted to keep nor was able to keep. And Paul sees the demands from without being replaced by new desires implanted within. He has in mind no doubt what the prophet Jeremiah spoke of in chapter 31:33 when he was prophesying a new covenant, concerning which God said through him 'I will put my law in their inward parts and write it in their hearts'. The demands of a law from without simply brought despair and bondage: the desires for the law from within brought release and liberty. Surely this liberating experience is supremely relevant today, for the heart of the problem of mankind is not a lack of knowledge of what is right but a lack of desire to do what is right. Paul could not bear to think of Christians going back again into the kind of bondage that man had known under the Old Dispensation. And so writing to the Galatians, chapter 5:1 he says 'Stand fast in the liberty wherewith Christ has made us free' and in Galatians 5:18 he speaks of the Christian as being 'not under the law'. Not under the law as far as getting right with God is concerned, and no longer left helpless under the demands of the law as far as living a life that is pleasing to God was concerned, but now having an enabling Holy Spirit creating new desires which would make the law his delight. And so Paul goes on to speak not only of the liberating experience under the New Covenant but also of:

(b) *The tranforming experience* In v.18 he speaks of a present and new glory. The glory that is revealed in the lives of those in whom the Holy Spirit dwells and in whom the Holy Spirit moves and works. Paul sees a vivid contrast here between the experience of Moses who veiled his face in the presence of men in order to conceal the glory that was fading from his face and the Christian who meets and gazes at the Lord with unveiled face and is being changed. Something of the moral splendour and righteousness which is resident in the nature and character of God will now be displayed in the life of the Christian in whom the Spirit of God dwells, and so he is being changed into 'His likeness'. This is one of the most tremendous statements that Paul has ever made about the Christian life. Salvation is regarded by Paul first of all as *a gift* but also as *a growth.* Salvation is not only a person but also a process, and the process is defined here in these tremendous words – that the Christians 'are being changed into His likeness from one degree of glory to another'. In other words, the Christian is becoming more and more like the Lord Himself Who said 'I delight to do Thy will, Oh God'. So Paul has spoken of *The Excellence of the Past Seen By Him: The Relevance Of The Truth Preached By Him* and he goes on to speak of:

C. THE EXISTENCE OF A FOE FEARED BY HIM

In chapter 4:4 Paul speaks of the god of this world having 'blinded the minds of those who believe not' 'those who refuse to believe' as Professor Barclay translates that final phrase. The Christian so often forgets the existence of the Devil but Paul was too aware of his activity ever to make that mistake. And so behind all the problems and difficulties in the situation at Corinth, and indeed in the Church everywhere, Paul realises that there are subtle spiritual forces at work, hostile to the Spirit of God. And it is within this context that Paul speaks of:

(a) *The refusal that is perilous* He warns against an attitude of mind which gives the Devil an opportunity to do his work; and his work is to blind our minds, to take away our sight, to take away our sensitivity to truth and to light. And the attitude is described by him as a 'refusal to believe'. This does not refer simply to those who reject Christ initially as the Saviour but it refers to an attitude of mind which allows the Devil to do his deadly work. If we adopt the attitude of being unwilling to respond to God's truth whether it is the saving truth of the gospel or whether it be some further light that God would shed upon our way; if our attitude is one of rebellion this gives the Devil the opportunity to come in and blind our minds, take away our sight, deaden our sensitivity to truth. How often one has seen this in experience. A person who is not a Christian comes to a service, they hear the gospel, they are profoundly disturbed, they feel they ought to accept Christ but then they think differently and the refusal, the attitude of rejection begins to form until it hardens. And that person who was once profoundly disturbed by the truth as it is in Christ can quite easily go into a gospel service again and remain quite unmoved. What has happened is simply that they have given the opportunity to the Devil to blind their minds. This can also happen in the life of a Christian who at one time has been extremely sensitive to God's truth and God's will, and by this refusal to believe, to respond, to obey, finally has grieved the Holy Spirit to such a measure that he becomes insensitive to His touch. The tragedy about sin whether in the life of the non-Christian or the Christian is that the more we sin the less we feel it to be sin. What greater tragedy in life than that a person who has seen should find themselves going blind. The refusal that is perilous: but also Paul speaks of:

(b) *The removal that is possible* People in that state he says are in danger. He describes them in chapter 4:3 as 'perishing'. This does not necessarily mean that their case is hopeless but it simply describes the course upon which they are travelling. But in chapter 3:16 he indicates where hope can be found. There we read 'when a man turns to the Lord the veil is removed' or in other words the attitude determines the experience. This is Paul's way oj stating what our Lord said in the Sermon on the Mount 'Blessed are the pure in heart for they can see God.' It is when a man turns to the Lord, when he adopts the attitude of willingness, of openness to Christ that the sight is restored and the veil is removed and the Lord is seen in all His splendour and glory. We want therefore to be careful and watchful lest the Devil is given an opportunity to blind our minds whether we are Christians or not, and let us never forget that the attitude will determine the experience. If we have already made up our minds concerning God's will and God's truth then the Devil will seize upon that and take away our sight. But in spite of the existence and activity of the Devil, Paul goes on to speak finally in this section of:

D. THE CONFIDENCE IN THE LORD SHOWN BY HIM

And his confidence is revealed in two ways: first of all he speaks of:

(a) *The vision he had seen for himself.* And so in chapter 4:6 he speaks of 'God who commanded the light to shine . . . hath shined in our hearts' Behind all that he had done, behind the whole emphasis and stress of his life, behind all his activity and preaching, there was this original initial experience of his encounter with Christ on the Damascus Road when the light had shined in his heart revealing Christ as the fulfilment of the law and the One who met every requirement of human need. Paul could never get away from the sense of wonder and worship that had filled his heart then as he thought of the mercy of Christ who was then revealed to him. And it was this Christ he preached – not himself. What a comfort those words are in v.5 'For what we preach is not ourselves but Jesus Christ as Lord; with ourselves as your servants for Jesus' sake'. This is a great encouragement to those of us who feel we are such inadequate and imperfect Christians. Some people hold back from Christian service because they feel they are not good enough. But of course the truth is that none of us is good enough, but we are not asked to be. We don't preach ourselves: the subject of our witness is Jesus Christ. And back of this testimony that we want to bear to Him is the consciousness of the reality of the experience of Him in our own lives. It is this that gives us confidence. Like the man whose eyes had been opened by the Lord 'one thing I know whereas I was blind now I see' and nothing could shake him from that position. The confidence of Paul is shown not only in his reference to the vision he had seen but also:

(b) *The verdict he must seek from others* Because Paul is so sure of his Lord, so sure in his own life of the relevance of the message that he preaches, so sure of the greater glory of the New Covenant as compared with the Old, he is passionately concerned that others should enter into this experience. So in chapter 4:2 he speaks of commending ourselves 'to every man's conscience in the sight of God'. Paul's task is not one of entertainment, not even instruction, but response. He is aiming at the conscience of men not only that they should recognise his own integrity and his own sincerity but that they should recognise the authority behind his words – an authority which is not his but God's, an authority to which they must respond either in obedience or in rejection. And all that he does is done 'in the sight of God'. So we find Paul beginning to move rather more positively and indeed with a hint of aggression.

The people in Corinth who had caused trouble had now apparently seen differently and there had been a change of heart and Paul is now seeking to build positively upon this encouraging news that there was a change of attitude, there was a difference in their relationship to him. And Paul wants to let them see now not simply an explanation of what his own reaction had been to the situation that was past but he wants to make a positive affirmation concerning the way in which the New Covenant so wonderfully and completely transcends the Old. This is another reflection or aspect or illustration of the words of St. Paul elsewhere 'If any man be in Christ he is a new creature; old things are passed away; behold, all things are become new'.

QUESTIONS FOR DISCUSSION

Study No. 4 – II Corinthians 3:4–4:6

1. There is a story told of a little girl who said to her mother, – 'Why is it that something inside me wants to do wrong?'
   How might we explain to a young person that this problem is dealt with under the New Covenant?
2. Consider the activities of the 'god of this world' as they are referred to in this section, and how they can be countered.
3. 'We must move with the times, jazz up our music and jazz up our message before we can expect to achieve anything.'
   Consider this view and Paul's statement 'by the *open statement* of the truth we would commend ourselves to every man's conscience in the sight of God.'
4. Certain words and phrases are predominant in this passage – notably 'confidence, hope, ministry'.
   What is, or should be, the reason for our confidence, the result of it, and the nature of our ministry?

Chapter 5

BATTLE AND BLESSING

Passage studied II Corinthians 4:7–15

This next section though short is full of revealing truths and facets of the experience of anyone engaged in the service of God, any who are prepared to open their mouths and give their witness and testimony to the faith in their hearts, their faith in Jesus Christ! There are three aspects of this conflict that Paul sets forth. We see first of all:

A. THE INSTRUMENT HE WAS

v.7 'we have this treasure in earthen vessels to show that the transcendent power belongs to God and not to us' or J. B. Phillips translation 'this priceless treasure we hold, so to speak, in a common earthenware jar – to show that the splendid power of it belongs to God'. There are two things here as clear as crystal:

(a) *The poverty of his life*. Paul describes himself here as 'a common clay pot'. What comfort there is here and also what caution. The mistake that so many of us make is that of thinking that the only people God uses in His service are those who think highly of themselves, and that unless we think we are wonderful Christians God can't use us. All the time the very reverse is the case. Christians who are greatly used do not think they are wonderful, they realise and know that they are worthless and useless, they are of no value at all, just 'common clay pots'. As Professor Tasker points out Paul knew he was a 'chosen vessel' Acts 9:15 but he also knew that he was 'an earthen vessel'. All this is in keeping with the whole trend of scripture. In the first chapter of I Corinthians v.27 following Paul writes 'God chose what is foolish in the world to shame the wise; God chose what is weak in the world to shame the strong'. Two things always marked Paul's estimate of himself. The first was amazement that God should ever have chosen him and abasement in the light of the knowledge of what God had done through him. Do you recall this abiding sense of wonder as recorded in Ephesians 3:8 'Unto me who am less than the least of all saints, was this grace given, that I should preach among the Gentiles the unsearchable riches of Christ'. One would have thought that such a priceless message conveying such a priceless truth would surely have had somebody very special to proclaim it and to convey it to men. Somebody more able, somebody more worthy; but no, God wanted to use 'clay pots'. If this be so then there is hope for us, for us who know that we are just ordinary Christians; that ordinary people are the very people that God wants to use. What a tremendous comfort there is here for those of us who think we are ordinary, and what a word of caution there is here for those who think they are rather extra special. And so Paul begins by stressing the poverty of his life and closely related to this:

(b) *The purpose of his Lord.* There is method in the madness of God; there is a reason for this and Paul states it. It is 'to show that the transcendent power belongs to God, and not to us'. Such a plain container will neither distract from the glory of the gift nor will it detract from the glory of the giver. You don't pay much attention to the paper in which a gift is wrapped up if it is plain brown paper. You concentrate entirely on the gift and the giver, these are the important things – not the brown paper that wrapped up the gift. This is so in the Gospel. Paul did not want people either distracted from the glory of God's gift in Christ or did he want to detract from the glory of

God's grace and mercy in him. And so the person who brings the gift and proclaims the truth is better to be just an ordinary person. When a ring is to be displayed it is usually against the background of a plain cloth. It may be a dark green cloth or a black cloth but it is always plain; it is not ornate, it is not embroidered heavily with elaborate patterns of gold or silver but plain cloth. And Paul sees the saving truth of God in Christ proclaimed by plain ordinary people. The saving power of Christ is displayed against this kind of background, and so the glory will obviously then go where the glory is due. Scripture tells us that God will not give His glory to another, and so we find that He delights to use ordinary people and the watching world gives the praise and the glory to God to whom it is due. What comfort there is for us in all this. So many of us feel so weak, and that's exactly what God wants us to be. So weak that God Himself is the only explanation of what we are able to do, what we are able to say, how we are able to live. The instrument he was. And then secondly in this section we see:

B. THE BEWILDERMENT HE FELT

To be on the side of God, to be on the side of goodness and of righteousness proved to be unexpectedly tough and difficult. This is a strange but frightful condemnation of human nature, namely, that with human nature goodness is not popular and not wanted. The reason of course is quite simple – sin pays and pleases men and when goodness comes along it just gets crucified. The next two verses are vivid in the terseness of the language and in the picture of the conflict. In the A.V. we read it thus, 'we are troubled on every side, yet not distressed; we are perplexed, but not in despair; persecuted, but not forsaken; cast down, but not destroyed'; There is contrast here, all through. First of all we see:

(a) *The onslaught.*

A.V.	R.S.V.	J.B.P.	W.B.	N.E.B.
Troubled	Afflicted	Handi-capped	Sore pressed	Hard pressed
Perplexed	Perplexed	Puzzled	At our wits end	Bewildered
Persecuted	Persecuted	Persecuted	Persecuted	Hunted
Cast down	Struck down	Knocked down	Knocked down	Struck down

What an amazing array of vivid phrases and what a battering this Christian had endured and every Christian must therefore expect. To expect anything else indeed is foolishness. The life of Christian service means being attacked and being assailed. The devil will see to it; the world will see to it; and the flesh, the human nature in ourselves or in others, including other Christians, will see to it as well. The Christian apparently is going to be hard pressed, hunted, bewildered struck down. Who was it who said, 'what are soldiers for but to be shot at.' And you and I must never be surprised when we find the Christian life to be a tremendous conflict and battle. We must never be surprised when we find we are assailed, attacked, tempted, and tried. But we see not only the onslaught but we see also:

(b) *The outcome*. There are four 'buts' in the four contrasts and we must never forget the 'buts' that faith puts in. Hard pressed – but – not hemmed in, or as J. B. Phillips translates it 'never frustrated'. Professor Barclay puts in this telling phrase 'there is always an element of spaciousness in the Christian life'. The forces of evil and of men may seem to press hard upon us and around us but there is a wider world of spiritual usefulness, of influence, of values, of realities, in which the Christian can roam freely however hardpressed he may be in his own personal circumstances. No Christian is ever finally or fully restricted by age, illness, or hatred. He may be hard pressed but he is never hemmed in. There is always another world of reality in which he can roam freely.

Perplexed - but - not in despair. At our wits end - but - not at our hopes end. When every human resource or reason is exhausted there are other resources and other reasons to bring to bear upon the situation. I remember hearing an American preacher say that he had met so many Christians who had 'run out of gas' i.e. petrol. But as far as Paul was concerned wherever he went he had a spare tank! He was perplexed - but - never in despair: persecuted - but - not forsaken. Persecuted by men but never abandoned by God. The N.E.B. translates this word 'hunted'. The Revised Version 'pursued'. Hunted, but never abandoned. There can be an element of ruthlessness about the way in which the servant of God will be got at by others. It may be in the office. There will be somebody who literally seems to persecute, to hurt, to pursue, the Christian - to take an almost fiendish delight in getting at him or at her. But we must remember that although we may be persecuted, or hunted, or pursued by them, we are never abandoned by God, and that right in the thick of the battle the Lord is always with us. Pursued and hunted - but - never abandoned by God. What a thrill that is. Joan of Arc said, 'it is better to be alone with God; His friendship will not fail me, nor His counsel, nor His love. In His strength I will dare and dare and dare until I die.' Cast down - but - not destroyed. J. B. Phillips translates this so wonderfully and matchlessly 'knocked down, but not knocked out'! We may fall, but we rise to fight again and to fight on. The Christian may lose a battle, but he goes on to win the war. 'Knocked down, but not knocked out.' The Christian never gives in to despair nor does he give way in defeat. I wonder how many of you know the poem that is titled 'Keep Me From Turning Back'. The words have often stimulated and challenged me.

'Keep me from turning back.
My hand is on the plough, my faltering hand,
But all in front of me is untilled land;

The wilderness and solitary place;
The lonely desert and its inter-space.
What harvest have I but this paltry grain:
These dwindling husks and handfuls of dry corn;
These poor lean stalks. My courage is outworn.
Keep me from turning back.
The handles of my plough with tears are wet,
The shares with rust are spoiled, and yet,
And yet, Oh God, my God,
Keep me from turning back!'

The Christian must remember to put the 'buts' into the battle. THE INSTRUMENT HE WAS: THE BEWILDERMENT HE FELT: and finally:

C. THE FULFILMENT HE SAW

Paul could see that the pattern of his own life and experience had something in common with the pattern and experience of the life of his Lord. Six times in these verses the word 'Jesus' occurs and in each case there are two things to note:

(a) *The life laid down.* v.10. In St. John's gospel our Lord is recorded as saying 'The good shepherd giveth his life for the sheep' Not simply in the act of death but in the devotion that his task requires. A devotion which will not shrink from death, and which may indeed ultimately demand death. Paul here speaks of 'always carrying in the body the dying of Jesus' This can be interpreted *physically*. Professor Tasker comments 'Jesus had to spend much physical strength and spiritual energy in the service of others. He was relentlessly hunted down by his political and religious opponents. He experienced sleepless nights and exhausting days with nowhere to lay His head. It might indeed be said that the death that He ultimately died was but the final stage of a dying that had been continuous while He trod the way of obedience as the suffering servant of God.' There is a sense in which it could be true to say that very often the sheer hardship involved in

Christian service may shorten a man's life. How often this has happened and men have died young and early who would not have died as young or as early if they had not been spent in God's service. But this can also be interpreted *spiritually* in this sense that the obedience of Christ which brought Him to the Cross involved a dying, a dying to social popularity, a dying to material prosperity, a dying to personal desire, a dying to sin itself. To be the kind of messenger Christ needed was to live the kind of life that Christ lived - indeed to live the risen life that Christ now lived in him. The life laid down and:

(b) *The fruit brought forth.* Here Paul is concerned about the benefits that emerged out of this sacrificial life of service and conflict to which he had been called. It is the same principle enunciated by our Lord when He said 'Except a corn of wheat fall into the ground and die it abideth alone, but if it die it bringeth forth much fruit.' The fruit was two-fold. There would be fruit in his own life and also there would be fruit in the lives of others. And in the light of this all the conflict, all the suffering, all the battle was infinitely worth while. In v.11 Paul speaks of the purpose and result being 'so that the life of Jesus may be manifest in our mortal flesh' There is fruit to be seen in his own life. In v.12 he speaks of 'death at work in us but life in you' and in v.15 of it all being for 'your sake' And so there would be fulfilment and gain as a result of all this. The fruit of increasing Christian character in his own life and the fruit of conversion in the lives of others. And the ultimate end of it all, in v.15 'as grace extends to more and more people it may increase thanksgiving to the glory of God'. Paul sees the benefits of God's mercy and grace reaching from life to life as a result of his own suffering and his own conflict, and that this will turn into thanksgiving and praise that will bring honour and glory to his God and his Lord. And this ultimately is the purpose of his whole Christian life that God's name should be glorified. Do you remember how our Lord Himself said 'Herein is my Father glorified that ye bear much fruit' and whether the fruit be a fully developed mature Christian character or God's grace spreading to more and more people, in either way or in both ways God's name will be glorified. And what greater end could man achieve than this; for what is man's chief end but to glorify God and to enjoy him forever.

QUESTIONS FOR DISCUSSION

Study No. 5 – II Corinthians 4:7–15

1. 'I'm neither clever enough nor good enough to speak about Christ.'

   How would you answer such a statement, in the light of what Paul says about himself?
2. Consider the reasons for a Christian's being 'struck down', and the resources with which he can meet the situation.
3. Christ said: 'Unless a grain of wheat falls into the earth and dies, it remains alone; but if it dies, it bears much fruit.'

   Discuss the different ways in which a Christian may lose his life, and thereby bear fruit.

Chapter 6

THOUGHTS ON GROWING OLD

Passage studied II Corinthians 4:16–5:9

There is possibly nothing that makes a person feel that he is beginning to grow old so much as the feeling that the burdens he has to bear, the battles he has to fight are getting beyond his strength. Our last study was entitled 'BATTLE AND BLESSING' and the difficulties in the work were leaving their mark. You may recall in chapter 1:8 how Paul describes how utterly worn out he had been 'we were pressed out of measure, above strength, insomuch that we despaired even of life itself' or as J. B. Phillips translates it 'we were completely overwhelmed, the burden was more than we could bear, in fact we told ourselves that this was the end'. I suggested that the news from Corinth of the attitude of those there who were against Paul had proved possibly to be the last straw. The battle of the work and the burdens of the need had drained Paul and he was beginning to realise that he was not so young as he used to be. And so he thinks his thoughts aloud about this aspect that must, from time to time, assert itself in the mind of the servant who seeks to give his Lord his devotion and service. So first of all in this section Paul speaks of:

A. THE COURSE THAT NATURE TAKES

Chapter 4:16 'though our outward man perish, yet the inward man is renewed day by day'. There are two things to note here:

(a) *What Paul accepts* 'though our outward man perish'. Physically this body of ours is not going to last for ever;

in fact it does wonderfully well to last so long, and it does this because it carries within it its own replacement and repair service. Indeed we are told that every seven years or so our body completely renews itself. This would mean that at my age I have gone through eight bodies at least so far and I am beginning to get through my ninth body! But there seems to come a time when even the body itself runs out of spares. We discover that our sight is not so good; our hearing is not so good; we don't seem to have the same amount of energy; we can't walk so far; we can't do so much. In Paul's case all this had been accelerated by the hardships he had endured in his service for Christ. And how true this can be that the service of God can make physical demands that shorten a man's life. Do you recall the advice of Jethro to Moses recorded in Exodus 18? Jethro had visited Moses and had seen the work that he was trying to do. In v.13 of that chapter we read how 'the people stood by Moses from the morning unto the evening'. As Jethro saw the tremendous burden that Moses was attempting to carry he protested 'The thing that thou doest is not good. Thou wilt surely wear away . . . this thing is too heavy for thee.' And so it was that Moses was told by Jethro to appoint others 'to bear the burden with thee'. It was not just the work that he was undertaking, it was the worry and the warfare. What Paul calls in v.17 'his light affliction'. As a matter of fact Paul was just getting worn out. And this was something I find that Paul was prepared to accept. Paul does not live and work as if he would do it for ever. His outward man was perishing. But although we see here what Paul accepts, we also see:

(b) *What Paul asserts*. While all that Paul had to say about the outward man perishing was true, it was not the whole truth, it was not the whole picture. The inner man, the real spiritual man was being renewed day by day. Or in other words while physically Paul was getting weaker spiritually Paul was getting stronger. This is one of the excitingly different things about being a Christian – you keep on growing spiritually. Physically a person can reach the point where he stops growing but spiritually he never does. The body may get worn out and old but not the man who dwells within the body. Inside, although he doesn't get younger, he doesn't stop growing. The Christian keeps on growing in his experience of God's ways, in his knowledge of God's Word, in his likeness to God's Son, in his usefulness in God's work, in his conformity to God's will. There is always development, there is always progress, in the life of a Christian. How sharply in contrast is the attitude about growing old if a person is not a Christian. Life becomes more and more restricted; the person is able to do less and less; so many of the things to which his energies have been devoted then begin to take on their true value; and the verdict that is passed here is so true 'the things that are seen are temporal; the things that are not seen are eternal'. The whole area of life which has been of value to the person who is not a Christian is something which is passing away. But the Christian lives in quite a different atmosphere. The approach of old age begins to throw his life into a true perspective and a new evaluation, and the unseen things which have occupied his mind are found to be not temporal but eternal.

And so Paul as a Christian man very sensibly takes note of The Course That Nature Takes and everybody whether a Christian or not would be wise to do the same. And then next we see here:

B. THE CHANGE THAT DEATH BRINGS

And the change is in the kind of body we have. This at least is the generally accepted interpretation of the verses that follow in the opening section of chapter 5. The present earthly and physical body that we have now Paul describes as:

(a) *A Pilgrim Shelter*. He calls it a tent – that is what the word tabernacle means. A tent is ideal for a journey. I can take a tent with me where I certainly couldn't take a house. And so this body is suited to this life that I live here on earth. A life which incidentally is thought of habitually in the Christian sense as being a journey or a pilgrimage. One of our hymns puts it like this:

> 'Here in the body pent,
> Absent from Him I roam;
> Yet, nightly pitch my moving tent
> A day's march nearer home.'

This thought of the Christian life as being a pilgrimage is of course found again and again in Scripture. Compare Hebrews 13:14 'here we have no continuing city, but we seek one to come'. Compare I Peter 2:11 where Peter describes the Christians to whom he writes as 'pilgrims and strangers.' This body that we have now is suitable for our earthly journey but not suitable for our permanent and eternal home. As we think of the Christian life as a pilgrimage or a journey it is worth pausing to recall what sights we have seen; what people we have met; and what experiences we have known. But if the Christian life is a journey, like all other journeys, it must have had its starting place. For Paul this was on the Damascus Road, and what a day that had been for him. All of us must have had a starting point for our Christian and spiritual pilgrimage. But if a journey has its starting place it also has its finishing point. And the journey of the Christian is a journey that will ultimately bring us home to God. But a change would come at death: the pilgrim shelter would be laid aside and it would be replaced by:

(b) *A Permanent Structure.* From what we can glean from Scripture there will be the same design in our new resurrection body but the fabric of which the body will be made will be different. We do not know too much about it. All we do know is that some tremendous change will take place. Everything that speaks of weakness and weariness, of sin and suffering will be gone. Paul describes it here as 'a building of God, eternal in the heavens, a house not made with hands'. We need a different body, we need a suitable body, suited to eternity and heaven. Do you remember in I Corinthians 15:35 following, where Paul uses the illustration of a seed sown in the soil; he likens death to this. There is obviously a connection between the seed and the resulting flower but there is also a difference. And then it is that Paul lists the characteristics of our mortal body and contrasts them with our new body. Instead of being marked by corruption the new body will be marked by incorruption: instead of mortality there will be immortality: instead of dishonour there will be glory: instead of weakness there will be power: instead of a natural body we shall have a spiritual body. The thought is so tremendous and the change so dramatic that we find Paul actually longing for it. This is brought out in v.4 where he writes 'For we that are in this tabernacle do groan, being burdened'. How different Paul's attitude was to death from the attitude of so many people today, even Christian people. We are told that today death is a topic that is never discussed by anybody if they can avoid it. Paul's attitude as a Christian was entirely different. Death was something that he anticipated with eager delight. Writing to the Philippians in his letter, chapter 1:23 he writes 'I am hard pressed between the two' that is to say between dying and remaining alive: and then he adds 'my desire is to depart to be with Christ'. A body we must have for thus our individuality is preserved and our recognition of one another in glory is assured. But if we must have a body we must have a different body. The present body is suited to earth, it is not suited to heaven. And so with some mysterious but vital connection between the old and the new a tremendous change will take place. As Paul says elsewhere 'we shall all be changed'.

I have never forgotten in my own family experience when on the day of the funeral of my elder sister who had died in her late twenties my father and I said farewell to all that was mortal before we went upstairs to the drawing room for the short service before setting out for the Church. My sister had been in great pain and suffering for between two and three years, and as we said farewell knowing that it was the last time we would look upon her mortal body my father said 'with another body next time, thank God'. As far as we can tell the body that we shall have in heaven will be like the resurrection body of Christ. This will be the change that death will bring.

And so Paul, thinking of growing old, thinks of THE COURSE THAT NATURE TAKES: THE CHANGE THAT DEATH BRINGS: and finally:

C. THE COURAGE THAT FAITH SHOWS

Twice over in the opening section of chapter 5 we have in the A.V. v.6 'Therefore we are confident' v.8 'we are confident'. The R.S.V. translates 'we are of good courage'. All that Paul has been saying up till now he has found to be of tremendous practical help to him in the present situation. It gave him courage to endure; just as the thought of a good fire and a cup of tea might keep us going when we were tired out after a long walk. There are two things that Paul has in mind as this section is brought to a close:

(a) *The principle by which the Christian lives has its limitations*. The Christian lives by faith – chapter 5:7. We only have in a sense the engagement ring now, we are not married. This is a legitimate interpretation of v.5 where Paul writes of 'the earnest of the Spirit'. The word translated earnest there is used of an engagement ring. Paul points out that while in a sense we have the presence of the Lord now, the Lord is present to faith and not to sight; and therefore in another sense, as far as sight is concerned, we are absent from the Lord. It is wonderful to walk with someone in the dark, it is much more wonderful to walk with them in the sunshine. The analogy that might help would be this: supposing somebody had been born blind, a child, brought up with love and affection, they would know so much about a mother's love and a mother's care but the child would not know what the mother looked like. Supposing this child was then able to have an operation and get the sight that it had never known, what a thrill to see the face of the mother who had cared and loved that child throughout all those years of blindness. So it will be with faith. There is a limitation that faith cannot transcend but that limitation will one day be brought to an end. And so Paul goes on to speak of:

(b) *The prospect for which the Christian looks has its motivation.* Now the prospect is the prospect of being present with the Lord, and because of this the Christian's whole concern is whether here or there his life should be pleasing to the Lord. v.9 'that, we may be accepted of Him'. We have been busy for Him here on earth and we are hurrying home with the work that we have done. We have tried to do it in such a way as will please Him, and now we are going to show it to Him to see whether or not He is pleased. The picture that comes to my mind is that which is so familiar to parents with children at school. The end of term comes: all during the term the children have been busy with their handwork and handcrafts. The boy may have been busy with his joinery, and the girl with her knitting; and now at the end of term the work that has all been done is being brought home, brought home so excitedly and so proudly to show to Mummy and Daddy. Every mother has things tucked away that have been made by her children at school. In the making of them the child has always had in mind the thought of making something that would be acceptable and pleasing to Mummy or Daddy. At the end of term, at the end of school, the gift is finally brought home for their inspection and approval.

This is Paul's attitude to death. It is something that he

anticipates with keen delight. The moment when, having been in a sense absent from the Lord, he will be present with Him.

I have never forgotten some lovely words that Mr. R. Hudson Pope gave to me, words that he found in the Bible of his mother after she died. This is how the verses run:

'My work for the day is almost through.
Was it all as in His sight?
Would Jesus be able to say, "well done"
Supposing He came tonight!

'There's a tiny sin on my soul today,
And I can't make my face look bright.
Would Jesus ask, "aren't you glad I've come?"
Supposing He came tonight.

'Lord Jesus, I want more grace each day
To help me to walk aright,
So that my heart may welcome You
Supposing You came tonight.'

QUESTIONS FOR DISCUSSION

Study No. 6 – II Corinthians 4:16–5:9

1. Consider the different attitudes to old age in the Christian and the non-Christian, and the opportunities that still exist for the older Christian.
2. Elsewhere Paul said: 'My desire is to depart and be with Christ, for that is far better.'
   Consider some of the ways in which it is 'far better'.
3. Consider the encouragement Paul derives, and the incentive he finds in his thinking on growing old.

Chapter 7

THE PRESSURE OF RESPONSIBILITY

Passage studied II Corinthians 5:9–6:10

This passage of scripture is simply packed full of truth and we could pause for long enough on any single verse. It always reminds me of what we used to call Scotch Bun. Scotch Bun in contrast to currant loaf is absolutely packed full of fruit, not the occasional currant as you might find in a currant loaf but simply solid fruit. This passage is simply solid truth. The connection with what has gone before is twofold. Our last study gave us Paul's thoughts on growing old. The thought of death is inevitably linked up in the mind of Paul with the thought of judgment. The thought of judgment immediately suggests to the mind of Paul the burden of responsibility that the Christian bears. The kind of inner pressure of responsibility, of obligation, of duty, of which a critic or onlooker or enemy is totally unaware. Paul has been saying a great deal about the outward pressures. Two studies back our title was 'Battle and Blessing' but now he is getting on to the inner pressures of which other people might know nothing. As we have pointed out before, in this letter we are allowed to see and sense more of the inner mind and thought of the apostle than in any other epistle. He has had so much to say about the battles he has had to fight; battles of which others might be aware but now he lets his readers see something of the burdens that he bears of which others know nothing. The burden, the pressure, of responsibility. Paul sees the responsibility of the Christian engaged in the service of his Lord as being viewed from three points of view. He sees:

A. HIS RESPONSIBILITY TO A MASTER

His accountability to his Lord. We see this thread of truth and thought running right through this section. Chapter 5:9 'that we may be accepted of him' chapter 5:10 'we must all appear before the judgment seat of Christ' chapter 5:11 'what we are is known to God' and in chapter 5:16 he warns of another and more superficial way of assessing a person, he speaks of knowing a person 'after the flesh'. Chapter 6 v.4 he writes 'in all things approving or commending ourselves as the ministers or servants of God' Paul was not a Christian just for the fun of it. The fact of his accountability to his Lord was something that was never far from his mind. He continually thought of his responsibility to his Lord who had done so much for him, who had given so much to him and now who asked so much from him. In thinking through his responsibility to Christ as a responsibility to a Master Paul has two things in mind:

(a) *The motives that actuated his service* and there were two. First of all there was the motive of fear – mentioned in v.11. The word translated 'terror' in the A.V. is translated more accurately 'fear' in the R.S.V. The fear that motivated and actuated Paul in his service was not the fear of what God might do to him if he failed but the fear of what he might do to God. The fear of hurting God, of disappointing Him. What an incentive this kind of fear has always been in our lives. We see it operating in our ordinary families. The fear in the heart of a child of disappointing a parent who is watching it, in a concert, playing a game in a team. I remember vividly when I used to play cricket for my school one of the thoughts that I always had was that I wanted to do well so that I would not disappoint the hopes of my father and whenever I saw him appear in the playing field, walking and strolling round the boundary line, this motivation immediately became powerful in my thinking. But if we feel like this for an earthly parent what about our spiritual family. What hopes the love of our Heavenly Father cherishes for us His children. He wants us to succeed, He wants us to win others for Himself; He wants us to serve well; He wants us to grow up into responsible, mature Christians; and the fear of disappointing the love of God is one of the most powerful motivations in Christian service. The second motive was 'love'. Paul speaks in v.14 of the compulsion of love 'the love of Christ constraineth us'. In the Greek the same word is used for constrain in this verse of St. Paul as the word used by our Lord Himself in Luke 12:50 'I have a baptism to be baptised with; and how am I straitened, or constrained, till it be accomplished!' Here was a love that drove Paul along almost irresistibly even as the love of Christ drove Him onwards to the cross. A love that was a caring concern for the good of others and for the glory of his Lord. It was this love that motivated his actions and dominated his living. We want to note exactly what the scripture states here. Paul was not speaking of his love for Christ but the love of Christ in him. This ties up with what he records in Romans 5:5 'the love of God is shed abroad in our hearts by the Holy Spirit which is given to us'. This quality of love means a total indifference to our own interests, and instead a concern that is wholly involved in the interests of others. Love's desire is to be with the ones loved, to share with those it loves all that it has to give, to serve, to work, to please others. These were the motives that actuated him. But in thinking of his responsibility to his Lord as a responsibility to a Master Paul thinks not only of the motives that actuated him but of:

(b) *The moment that awaited him* v.10. The moment of true assessment: there he records 'we must all appear before the judgment seat of Christ'. This was not an assessment that the Christian feared but an assessment that the Christian would want, and for which he waits with longing and desire. The peril of this Church, as of any Church, is found if assessments are false. And so he refers in v.12 to those who 'glory in appearance, and not in heart'. Paul says that the whole of his life *now* lies open to God; its motives; its ambitions; its successes; its failures. v.11 'to God we are already known through and through'. But when that day of assessment comes then the final and true verdict will be passed upon the worth of his life and ours. His detractors did not think the way God thought, they did not know what God knew, they did not even want what God wanted. They judged after the flesh and their judgments were therefore invalid. Paul was trying in this letter to share so much more of the inner conflicts, the inner pressures, the hidden motives, the secret sorrows, that his friends at Corinth might be able to understand better. This would enable them incidentally to speak out on his behalf not for his glory but for the sake of the work and for the glory of his Lord. And this is what Paul is getting at in v.12. But as for Paul himself the only person that he was really concerned with was his Lord. There was no pretence in that direction; success or failure, ecstasy or despair, everything was open to the Lord nothing was concealed, and the reward of service in eternity would be based upon the whole truth and nothing but the truth as God would see it.

RESPONSIBILITY TO A MASTER. This is the first aspect of responsibility in the mind of Paul. The second aspect of responsibility we see here is:

B. RESPONSIBILITY FOR A MESSAGE

Chapter 5:14–6:2 Paul's thought of his accountability to his Lord led on inevitably to the consideration of the exact nature of that for which he was accountable. In I Thessalonians 2:4 he describes the Christian as 'put in trust with the gospel'. Like an ambassador we have a mission and a message and our responsibility is to see that the message is delivered. And so in v.18 Paul writes of the

God who has given to him 'the ministry of reconciliation' and in v.20 of himself and all other Christians as 'ambassadors for Christ' and in v.19 he speaks of 'the word of reconciliation'. There are two things to note concerning the message for which Paul felt himself to be peculiarly responsible. First of all we note:

(a) *The event of which the message speaks* and that event was the death of Christ. The Christian religion has at the heart of its message the fact of the death of Jesus Christ and in this death the message speaks of something God has done for man. The real heart of the Christian gospel is not that God is asking us to do anything for Him but rather that He has done something for us, something that needed to be done, something that need never be done again. And so we read in v.14 'one died for all' v.15 'he died for all' v.15b we read of 'him which died for them'. We need to remember that a fact of history lies at the basis of Christian faith, and this death of Christ had meaning and had a purpose. It was not simply the fact of the death of Christ that was the message but its content, its significance, and this is brought out very clearly in these verses. v.19 'God was in Christ reconciling the world unto himself' v.18 'God, who hath reconciled us to himself by Jesus Christ' v.20 'be ye reconciled to God'. The problem of all living is basically a problem of right relationships, and the cross is here related to the most basic relationship of all – the relationship between man and God; and through the death of Jesus Christ reconciliation between man and God has been made possible. God has done that which needed to be done in order to make reconciliation possible. Not only is God's love revealed in the cross but the law of God has been satisfied in and through the death of Christ. And so at the heart of this message for which Paul felt responsible lay the event of which the message spoke. And Paul is also aware of the fact of:

(b) *The effect to which the message leads*. Where this message was believed it was a transforming message. The whole person and his whole world are transformed, and so we read in v.17 'if any man be in Christ he is a new creature: old things are passed away; behold, all things are become new.' 'Old things are passed away,' then a whole lot will drop out of his life. 'Behold, all things are become new,' then a whole lot will come into his life that is new. He will be a new man living in a new world. The whole person is changed and also the whole pattern. In v.15 Paul writes of the death of Christ 'he died for all, that they which live should not henceforth live unto themselves but unto him which died and rose again.' 'Not henceforth unto themselves but unto him'. The whole pattern of life would be reorientated. The Christian is somebody who is concerned no longer with his own will but with God's will: not so much concerned about his own person as other people: not concerned so much about his own convenience as God's glory. There is a total reorientation of life when the message of the cross is believed and the love of Christ received. How desperate the need is for this kind of change in this crazy mixed up world in which we live, and the Christ of the cross can bring it to pass. Is it any wonder then that there is a note of urgency underlying what Paul is saying here! His language is strong. He speaks of 'we beseech you' and again 'now is the accepted time; now is the day of salvation'.

His responsibility was a RESPONSIBILITY TO A MASTER: a RESPONSIBILITY FOR A MESSAGE: and finally:

C. RESPONSIBILITY AS A MINISTER

Or as the word should read in chapter 6:4 'as a servant'. This final section covers II Corinthians 6:3–10 and there are two final thoughts that Paul stresses. The first is:
(a) *The endurance that we must not lack*. He speaks in v.4 of 'in all things approving ourselves as the ministers of

God, in much patience' or as it is more accurately translated 'through great endurance'. What is the responsibility of a servant? It is surely having been given a task to see that that task is finished. His responsibility then is to endure until the work is done. He is not to give up: he is not to give in. And so Paul sets this responsibility against the background of the directions from which will come difficulty; difficulty that has to be faced and endured. He speaks of the spiritual load – the internal conflict of the servant. He speaks of afflictions – the sheer weight of the need and the task weighing heavily upon the mind. He speaks of necessities – the experiences which are part of our human lot which we cannot escape which may affect our spiritual life: essential human experiences such as sorrow or anxiety but these are not to detract us from our faithfulness to our task. He speaks of distresses, frustrations. But in addition to the spiritual load there are the social reactions which can make it difficult for a servant to endure. For Paul these reactions from his fellowmen were startling. For us they may not take the same form but they will have the same animosity very often behind them. He speaks of stripes – actual physical pain inflicted by his fellowmen upon his body. It may be that our bodies are not lashed but it may be our spirits are lashed not with whips or scourges but with tongues and words. He speaks of imprisonment: this is still experienced physically in some countries where Christians are imprisoned for their faith; socially they are shut out from the life of the community and confined within the walls of a prison. But you need not be enclosed within the walls of a prison to be shut out from the social life of a community. How many Christians have known what it is to be excluded from the fellowship of others and friendship of others in an office and even in a church. Paul speaks of tumults – he was no stranger to the violence of mobs. It happened then, it could happen again. There are social reactions which make it difficult for the servant to endure, but his responsibility is to endure. The spiritual load, the social reactions and the personal disciplines. Paul speaks of labours – the sheer hard physical work, the mental effort involved in serving God. He speaks of watchings – the sleepless nights; the disturbed nights; the nights when he would be up late praying, counselling, seeking. He speaks of fastings – the going without food or other legitimate pleasures which he did not have time for, did not have money for. The spiritual load; the social reaction; the personal disciplines; all these made it difficult. The danger that Paul could see was the danger of failing to maintain a right standard and thus giving an excuse to others to reject the message he proclaimed. The Christian servant must endure and carry on whatever the situation may be until his Master releases him from the task. And so Paul speaks not only of the endurance that we must not lack but of:

(b) *The encouragement the Christian must not miss.* And the encouragement is twofold. The first is that he has the tools for the job and secondly he knows the truth about the job. How can he endure? How can he overcome? Well, there is a whole array of qualities that will be needed but they are within the reach of the child of God who is indwelt by the Holy Spirit of God and growing in grace and in the knowledge of God. Paul speaks of pureness – or a disinterestedness, singleness of purpose, motivation that is crystally clear and sincere. He speaks of knowledge – or as J. B. Phillips translates it 'insight' a sight that sees in, that sees beyond the outward; a sight, a mental awareness that is sensitive to human need and to divine truth. He speaks of longsuffering and the word used here means longsuffering particularly in relationship to people, people who are slow to learn or stubborn to yield, people who are stupid. It is sometimes said as if it was a compliment concerning a person that 'he does not suffer fools gladly.' That is never true of a Christian servant of God. He is prepared to be longsuffering even with fools. He speaks of kindness – an attitude towards others which is thoughtful and considerate, gentle, which knows nothing of rudeness or roughness or harshness. Kindness is always winsome. He speaks of the Holy Ghost producing and maintaining all that there is of Christ in us. Of love unfeigned – an unaffected and genuine concern for others shown in our attitude towards them. The word of truth – a message which is true which is not our own and which we must reproduce accurately and truthfully and he speaks finally of the power of God – that power which is God's own prerogative, a power which can convict and convert others. The armour of righteousness on the right hand and on the left. Both for defence and for attack the Christian is well equipped. On the right hand he has *the sword of the spirit*; on the left hand *the shield of God's faithfulness*. He has the tools for the job and this is his encouragement. These tools are available to anyone in whom Christ dwells for they are all found in Him. But the other great encouragement lies in the truth that he knows. Paul here sets in a series of vivid contrasts the idea that the world has about a Christian servant and the picture that God has: *The world* – Dishonour; evil report; a deceiver; unknown; dying; chastened; sorrowful, poor; having nothing. *God* – honour; good report; true; well known; living; not killed; always rejoicing; making many rich; possessing all things. In fact the final verdict of the worldling is that the Christian really has nothing and yet the Christian knows perfectly well that he has everything.

And so it is with this truth that he is encouraged and upheld as he goes on in his service enduring to the end, knowing that one day he will discover that he has been RESPONSIBLE TO A MASTER: FOR A MESSAGE: AS A MINISTER.

QUESTIONS FOR DISCUSSION

Study No. 7 – II Corinthians 5:9–6:10

1. What should be the effect on our lives of the knowledge that we live under the judgment of our Heavenly Father?
2. 'God was in Christ, reconciling the world to Himself.' 'If any man is in Christ, he is a new creation.'

   Is this a good summing up of the Gospel message? How might we use these texts to explain the Gospel to an enquirer? In what ways might we say that *we* are a 'new creation'?
3. 'We are ambassadors for Christ.'

   Does an ambassador fail to promote his country's interests? Does he give his own opinion on a controversial issue? Does he act on his own authority? Does he find it strange to take orders from his government? Does he remain for long periods out of touch with his government?

   Consider Paul's summing up of the Christian life in the light of these questions.
4. What do we learn in 6:3–10 of 'the world's' attitude to the Christian, and the Christian's attitude to 'the world'?

Chapter 8

THE PRINCIPLE AND PRACTICE OF SEPARATION

Passage studied II Corinthians 6:11–7:3

We are drawing to the end of the first part of the Epistle, a part where Paul has been sharing with the Christians at Corinth something of the inner thoughts and pressures in his life and by this means he hoped to re-establish a measure of the confidence which had suffered through the activities of his traducers. This is hinted at in v.11 and 12 of chapter 6 and again in vv.2 and 3 of chapter 7. Professor Denney comments 'want of love and confidence between the minister of the gospel and those to whom he ministers has great power to frustrate the grace of God'. This is what Paul is hinting at in chapter 6:3 where we read, 'giving no offence' or as the R.S.V. translates it 'putting no obstacle in anyone's way'. Paul points out his own affection for them again. J. B. Phillips translates v.11 'Oh, our dear friends in Corinth, we are hiding nothing from you and our hearts are absolutely open to you'. This is what he had been doing right up to this very point, sharing with them all that he had been experiencing – the kinds of pressures he had known the very existence of which they could never have dreamed. This is of course what love does, what love longs to do. It longs to share its deepest thoughts with those it loves, and love wants to receive the same in return. And so J. B. Phillips goes on to translate v.12 'Any stiffness between us must be on your side, for we assure you there is none on ours. Do reward me with the same complete candour!' And again in chapter 7:2 comes the same plea 'open your hearts to us' ending with the lovely assurance 'as I said before, whether we live or die you live in our hearts'. Paul's love and affection are just spilling over and he wants, and he feels he is beginning to have, a response from them to match his own love for them. Paul longs for this mutual affection and confidence to be completely re-established. Happiness here will mean everything to him in his continued service, while unhappiness here will sap his strength as nothing else could. Professor Barclay comments, 'if a man is happy at home he can face up to anything outside his home; if a man is in fellowship with his friends he can withstand the slings and arrows of fortune with a smile'. How true these words are, and how true the opposite are – if a man is not happy at home, if a man is not in fellowship with his friends, then the outside pressures are trebly hard to bear. Paul sees the rain clouds are passing and the light is all the clearer for the rain. Denney comments thus 'The end of a quarrel between friends is like the passing away of a storm. The elements are meant to be at peace with each other and nature never looks so lovely as in the clear shining after rain.' I love that phrase 'the clear shining after rain'. Paul feels that the relationship between himself and the Corinthians is emerging into that clear shining after rain. The clouds of misunderstanding and criticism, of hostility, were like thunder clouds they were passing away and there was little left but the muttering of a distant faint echo, the clear shining after rain is almost here. And right in the middle of this section comes the passage which at first sight seems to have very little in common with what comes before it and after it. The passage beginning at v.14 in chapter 6 'Be ye not unequally yoked together with unbelievers'. So different is this felt to be that some commentators have gone so far as to suggest it doesn't really belong here, that a page from another letter has got mixed up with the pages of this letter. But this of course need not be so. The very awareness that the clouds were passing surely made Paul passionately concerned lest they should ever return; and so he inserts this plea for utter devotion and utter separation from everything that could spoil the relationship between a Christian and his Lord and the relationships between Christian and Christians. There is a sensitivity about love that hates anything that spoils the openness between two hearts in love with one another. There is a perfectionism about love: love's standard is tremendously high. I have always remembered what a mother once said to me about her daughter 'she is a perfectionist'. Her work had to be absolutely right, there had to be nothing slipshod about it, even if it was a Sunday School lesson for just a handful of children the lesson had to be prepared perfectly. The breach of fellowship that was now being healed had had its roots somewhere. It may have been from the old traditional Jewish side or it may be from the old immoral pagan side. But if there was to be no re-occurrence of the infection something would have to be done to insure that it never returned. And so Paul brings out here what I have called THE PRINCIPLE AND PRACTICE OF SEPARATION.

Separation is a word that has almost dropped out of the vocabulary and thought of Christians today. It was a word with which we were very familiar when we were young. It is of course something which is found in the Bible. Denney comments 'there is no conception of holiness into which the idea of separation does not enter'. And when we stop to think the same concept of separation 'from' and separation 'for' is found in other realms and walks of life. In the area of health and surgery, the instruments to be used are separated *from* any possible infection and they are separated *for* the work of healing for which they exist. In the realm of love and marriage the vow phrases it thus, 'and forsaking all other keep thee only unto her, only unto him, so long as ye both shall live'. Separated *from* others in order to be separated *to* the one to whom the person is now married. In the realm of industry and power the same principle applies. The power cables which straddle the countryside are all separated from the earth, insulators make certain that there is no contact between the power flowing through the cables and the earth. There are three things about separation that Paul speaks about here. First of all:

A. THE INCONSISTENCY AGAINST WHICH THEY ARE WARNED

vv.14 and 15. There is a word that has crept into our language and common speech; it is the word incompatibility. My dictionary defines this as 'incapable of existing together in harmony'. We use this word to describe how two people just cannot work together or live together – it may be in the realm of marriage or in business or it may be in the realm of the mission field. People just can't get on together. Like the oil and water they don't mix. Paul is warning the Christians at Corinth against attempting what will never work, either in marriage or in business or in Christian fellowship. We need to think back again into the background, how again and again paganism or Judaism would impinge on their way of life as new Christians. They needed to realise that there were some things quite irreconcilable in Judaism, in paganism, with the truth of God revealed in Christ and with the character of God revealed in Him. Paul notes two things:
(a) *How attractive such compromise might appear*. In every walk of life this is so. It could be financially: to lower their Christian standards might hold the promise of financial gain. It could happen socially: to compromise their code of conduct might hold the promise of greater social acceptability it may be from people who seemed important people. Emotionally, to marry an unbeliever might hold the promise of fulfilment and of enjoyment. How attractive compromise can seem. But Paul notes:
(b) *How deceptive such connections would prove*. Spiritually

and morally there would be a basic incompatibility. 'What fellowship' says the A.V. 'what partnership' R.S.V. 'what common interest' J. B. Phillips. How can these contradictory things ever coexist? Righteousness cannot coexist with unrighteousness: light cannot coexist with darkness. And then pushing behind the outward to the inward view of things. How can Christ coexist with Belial? How can faith coexist with unbelief? And then bringing it right home to themselves and their involvement in this situation – How can the temple of God be the place where idols are housed? Paul here is bringing home a very sensitive and jealously guarded sanctity with which all his readers would be familiar. For the temples of whatever faith were jealously guarded against desecration: indeed nothing was guarded more jealously and nothing, if violated, was more promptly and terribly avenged. Paul himself was nearly mobbed and ran the risk of his life when a rumour arose that he had taken an unbeliever into the temple at Jerusalem.

THE INCONSISTENCY AGAINST WHICH THEY WERE WARNED and then secondly there is also here in the mind of Paul the thought of:

B. AN INTEGRITY TOWARDS WHICH THEY MUST WORK

Whilst there is a negative side to separation there is a positive side too. They were to be separated *from* in order that they could be separated *to* and separated *for*. The negative side of the truth of separation is only the first step, after that there is work to be done and action to be taken and purposes to be fulfilled. Those sterilised surgical instruments are set aside in order that they may fulfil the ministry of healing; they are set aside for the use of the surgeon. Sterilisation is vital but it is only initial. They are not kept sterile simply for the sake of being sterile. They are kept sterile so that they can be used. And so in chapter 7:1 we read 'Having therefore these promises, let us cleanse ourselves from every defilement of body and spirit and make holiness perfect in the fear of God' or as the A.V. translates it 'perfecting holiness'. Make it your task to be a spiritually fit Christian. Was it not Robert Murray McCheyne who urged 'study universal holiness of life: your sermons last but an hour, your life preaches all the week'. What does all this mean? It would mean that they would have to be:

(a) *Personally disciplined.* There is a sense in which we have to learn to say 'no' to ourselves and 'no' to our Society, and this section is full of instructions, of imperatives, to be obeyed. Chapter 6:14 'Do not be mismated with unbelievers' chapter 6:17 'come out from among them, touch not the unclean thing' 7:1 'let us cleanse ourselves from every defilement'. When we become aware of something in our conduct or in our character that is inconsistent with the mind and will of God Paul says in effect 'cut it out'. The Christian life is one of continual discovery and therefore of continual progress. God takes us as it were from classroom to classroom. We learn more and more about ourselves, we learn more and more about our Saviour, we learn more and more about the society and world in which we live. And we are to live lives that are disciplined personally 'perfecting holiness'. But we are also to live lives that are:

(b) *Socially different.* 'Come ye out from among them, and be ye separate'. This means quite simply that there will be certain places where the Christian will not be found: there are certain people with whom the Christian will not associate: there are certain principles that the Christian will never entertain. Sometimes the separation may be actually physical, but certainly always morally and spiritually and mentally the Christian must be prepared to be different, to think differently and act differently.

THE INCONSISTENCY AGAINST WHICH THEY WERE WARNED: AN INTEGRITY TOWARDS WHICH THEY MUST WORK: and:

C. AN INTIMACY AT WHICH THEY WILL WONDER

Again the stress is positive. The Christian is separated *from* but also separate *to* and *for*. The surgeon is exacting in his requirements because he wants to heal the diseased body. Love is faithful to the one love because it wishes to be happy with that loved one. The power lines are insulated against becoming earthed so that the wheels of industry may move. And so we find the promise of God's intention and response to His requirement of separation 'I will live in them, I will walk in them, and they shall be my people' 'I will receive you and will be a Father'. Two things we can note as we close this study. First of all:

(a) *What God wants to do in us*. And there are two things – He wants first of all 'to live' and also 'to walk'. Not just to be there but to be free to go where He wants and to do what He likes. Sometimes we talk about being given the run of a place. By that we mean being allowed to go wherever we want and to do whatever we like. This is what God wants to do in us. He wants to have 'the run of the place' to be free to go wherever He chooses in our lives and to do whatever He wants with our lives. This is what God wants to do in us, and if He is going to do that in us then it is quite unthinkable for us to have everywhere things in our lives that would jar Him and hurt Him and grieve Him. God cannot be at home where He cannot be at home. That's worth thinking through. But also there is the thought here of:

(b) *What God wants to be to us*. 'And will be a Father, and ye shall be my sons and daughters'. The ultimate purpose of all God's saving grace is that there should be established a family fellowship with God as the Father. The Christian is to be the member of a great family, not a quarrelsome family but a family living together in harmony. Not a warring mob but a community where the Father's wealth provides what is needed; where the Father's wisdom plans what is best, and where the

Father's will directs the lives of those who are in the fellowship. But if this is going to be so, if this intimacy with God is going to be enjoyed, if this intimacy of fellowship is going to be enjoyed with one another then we must be separated from everything that would grieve Him and would hurt others in the family.

THE PRINCIPLE AND PRACTICE OF SEPARATION.

QUESTIONS FOR DISCUSSION

Study No. 8 – II Corinthians 6:11–7:3

1. Why is it important that fellowship between Christians, and between Christians and their Pastor should be unclouded?
2. 'I'm sure it's God's will for me to marry him, although he's not a Christian.'

   Would you agree with a Christian girl who said this? If you don't, how might you justify your disagreement?
3. 'It doesn't matter if a Christian has an odd drink, or an odd flutter on the horses.'

   Would Paul have approved of such a statement? Would such an attitude lead to the integrity which he advocated?
4. What is the intention of God, in and through His people, if they will separate themselves as His people?

Chapter 9

ALL'S WELL THAT ENDS WELL

Passage studied II Corinthians 7:4–16

This ninth study in Paul's second letter to the Church at Corinth ends the first section of the epistle. You will recall that the whole purpose of this has been to re-establish the bond of mutual confidence that had been apparently destroyed and endangered by Paul's detractors. These detractors may have been either those who were holding steadily to the Jewish traditions from which Paul had sought to set Christians free, or it may have been those who were attempting to compromise with pagan practices and standards and to retain these in their social and personal lives. Whatever the reason might have been Paul's influence had been endangered and his person had been under severe censure. Paul meets all this with a frankness that is intended to be disarming. He lets the Church see deeply into his own thoughts, his own reactions, his own sufferings, his own burdens and responsibilities. This final section, in chapter 7, is in a sense a kind of summary of the whole affair, ending as it opens with Paul's statement of his confidence in the Church. In v.16, the sentence which ends this part of the epistle, we read in the R.S.V. 'I rejoice because I have perfect confidence in you'. There are three facets of the whole unhappy event that Paul recalls and restates. First of all we see:

A. THE REBUKE ADMINISTERED BY PAUL

The major part of this section is concerned with the rebuke that Paul had administered by his letter referred to twice over in v.8, a letter of which we have no trace, the letter which Titus, in all probability, took with him to Corinth and concerning the reception of which Paul's mind had been filled with anxiety ever since! His anxiety had sent him hurrying in to Macedonia to await the return of Titus who possibly met him at Philippi. It had been a letter of censure and rebuke, and Paul had been anxious ever since as to how it had been received. Someone has said that an essential quality for leadership is 'the capacity to inflict pain' and Paul is displaying that quality in his leadership of the Church at Corinth. It is the same kind of capacity to inflict pain that will mark the work of a surgeon, of a nurse, of a dentist. Although I have been told by a relation of mine who is a dentist that with all the modern aids to dentistry nobody should ever suffer pain in the dentist's chair! But certainly we are aware of the fact that very often if there is to be healing there must be a hurting first. In administering this rebuke two things emerge. First of all:

(a) *The correction that their lives demanded.* It seems an obvious statement that every Christian and every church will need correction and rebuke but the tragedy is that so many Christians resent it when it comes their way. This is no new feature of life. Indeed if you turn back to the Proverbs, that book packed full of wisdom, you will find that there is a constant reference to this, the fact that a foolish man will resent blame and criticism while a wise man will gladly receive it and learn from it. I have noted with concern the way in which many evangelical Christians will gladly support a crusade, an evangelistic campaign, where the target area is the unconverted world. They will come gladly, they will support it regularly, they will be there in their place night after night; but the very same Christians who will support an evangelistic crusade, whose target area is the unconverted world, will stay away from a convention where the target area is the Christian Church, where the purpose is that Christians should become better Christians. It would seem as if this reflects precisely an element of peril in our whole attitude to truth. So often Christians don't want to be in the target area of the truth of God. It is too humbling, it is too disturbing, it is too demanding. This is why sometimes some people, some Christian people, will leave a church because the ministry is not simply the preaching of the Evangel, of the way *in* to the Kingdom of God, but it is the preaching of the whole biblical truth of the mind and will of God as concerning the Christian. This seems so stupid and so feeble but it is a fact that we have to face. One can expect it in the lives of those who are not Christians but surely it ought not to be found in the lives of those who are. Because if we are living our lives as they ought to be lived we will be living them under the constant judgment of God Himself. We will be so used to being criticised as it were by God that we will be prepared to take criticism from any quarter, and learn and profit by it. But Paul's concern was lest the Corinthian Church had failed to respond wisely to the rebuke that his letter had contained. But we see not only the correction that their lives demanded but also:

(b) *The compassion that his love displayed.* v.8 is very revealing. Here Paul speaks of himself as a man who knew he must rebuke but he does it with extreme reluctance and he does it with great concern. So we read in v.8 'For even if I made you sorry with my letter I do not regret it, though I did regret it, for I see that that letter grieved you, though only for a while'. Paul's concern and feeling for the Corinthian Church is shown not only by the reluctance, almost the regret that he had that he had ever written such a letter, but also by the anxiety with which he awaited news of the results of his letter. And so in v.5 he recalls how he could not stay in Asia, how he was so restless awaiting news from Titus that he made his way on to Macedonia no doubt to Philippi: and there difficulties without were matched by anxieties within. And so he says in v.5 'our bodies had no rest – fightings without and fear within'. Here is a man who cared deeply for those to whom he had had to administer rebuke. He had administered correction but he did it with extreme reluctance and with great tenderness and sensitiveness, and with compassion. I am sure that our experience would bear this out that when correction is administered with reluctance, when it comes from a person who very very seldom says anything that is in the nature of a rebuke the gentlest hint of censure is worse than a blow in the face. If somebody is always bawling, if somebody is always shouting, if somebody is always ticking people off we begin to harden our hearts and our minds against that harshness: but when a very gentle hint of censure or disappointment comes from somebody whom we know cares for us, someone who very seldom if ever speaks in that way, it cuts deeply. And so it had been at Corinth·

THE REBUKE ADMINISTERED BY PAUL: and then also in this section we see:

B. THE REASONS ASCRIBED

When rebuke is being administered the motives involved play an essential part. And Paul reveals in what he says here, first of all:

(a) *How spiritually he had acted* in v.12 'So although I wrote to you, it was not on account of the one who did the wrong, nor on account of the one who suffered the wrong (that is to say – himself) but in order that your zeal for us might be revealed to you in the sight of God'. Paul sweeps aside personalities. He is not concerned with the person or persons who had caused the trouble; neither is he concerned with himself, the person who had been most hurt by it. Personalities were irrelevant: spiritualities were important. He desperately wanted the old relationship of confidence re-established because if it was not re-established then his influence and his helpfulness as far as the Corinthian Church was concerned would be brought to an end. Paul was quite sure that it was there, that in the hearts of the vast majority of the Corinthians at Corinth there still was an attitude of confidence towards him, but it had become overgrown by the talk and the gossip, and the chatter, and the criticisms of those who opposed the message for which Paul stood. Rather like a building that had been overgrown with weeds and ivy until the original building was concealed, nevertheless the original building was still there. And so Paul's purpose in all that he had said was in order that the Christians at Corinth might rediscover their real condition, their real quality as Christians in the sight of God. This was his motive. He knew that until that relationship of mutual confidence had been restored he could not help them. This of course is true, whether it be in the relationship between a pastor and his congregation or between a Sunday School teacher and her class. Where that bond of confidence is destroyed there can be no communication, no blessing, no grace. So having stressed how spiritually he had acted Paul goes on to stress:

(b) *How sensibly they had reacted.* And here he makes a differentiation between what he calls godly grief and worldly grief. Godly grief views the situation in the light of God's truth, God's will, God's mind, God's grace, God's glory. And it was in this sense that they had reacted to the rebuke that Paul had administered. Such kind of grief, such kind of regret would be productive of salvation, that is to say it would be productive and positive in the sense that Christians who had been in need of rebuke would through correction find their way back into the path of God's grace and God's will. Worldly grief would be characterised by no basic change of mind; there might be regret but it would be remorse, it would not be repentance. It would be a concern not for the fact that they had sinned so much as a concern for the consequences that would follow on after that fact. The Church at Corinth had reacted sensibly and spiritually. They had viewed themselves in the sight of God. Personalities again had been lost to sight and the one basic relationship that mattered above every other relationship was the one by which they had viewed the whole series of incidents.

The reasons ascribed. We have seen in this section first of all then *The Rebuke Administered*: and then secondly, *The Reasons Ascribed*: and finally:

C. THE RESULTS ACHIEVED

What was the outcome of it all? Well, there was a twofold outcome. First of all we see:

(a) *His praise of the Church.* The man who had been compelled to speak about their failure now speaks equally frankly about their good qualities as reported by Titus. And so in v.7 and again in v.11 he enumerates these. Titus had spoken of 'their longing' for him – their desire to see Paul again. The people who had seemed at one time as if they were finished with him had now obviously indicated that they longed to have his help. Titus had spoken of 'their mourning' – their sorrow for the past, their deep regret at all that had been involved, at the hurt that they had caused, at the mistakes that they had made. And Titus also reported on 'their zeal' for Paul. Now they were ready to speak up for him; they were quick to move to his defence. Those who had been prepared to listen to his detractors were now no longer prepared to listen to that kind of talk. In v.11 he speaks of 'their indignation' – their indignation at the shame that they had brought upon the name of Christ, at the injury that they had done to the life and fellowship of the Church, at the peril into which they had entered through their foolishness, at the hurt they had caused. Titus also had noted 'their fear' – their alarm, of God's wrath, of God's displeasure to which they had exposed themselves: and also he notes 'their punishment' – their desire to punish and not to be deceived by the offender. It is a good thing to praise when there is ground for praise. There are some Christians, and evangelical Christians are possibly amongst the worst offenders, who are only too ready to find fault with others and desperately slow to show appreciation or to express thanks, or to give praise when praise is due. I wonder whether life would not be happier and brighter for us all in our Christian fellowships if there was a little more observation of points calling for praise, for commendation, for thanksgiving.

The other result that Paul indicates is not only his praise of the Church, but:

(b) *His pride in the Church.* He felt this very deeply and refers to this in v.4 where he writes 'I have great pride in you'. He not only felt it but he shared it, he had shared it with Titus. We see this referred to in v.14 where Paul writes 'For if I have expressed to him some pride in you, I was not put to shame; but just as everything we said to you was true, so our boasting before Titus has proved true'. His pride and his confidence in the Church at Corinth had not only been felt by him and shared by him but now it had been vindicated and confirmed. I remember very clearly some time ago having severe toothache. I was spending a holiday in the highlands of Scotland and I was far from the normal kind of services of a dentist. I was, however, told that a dentist came round on a certain day and conducted his surgery in a farmhouse. I remember turning up, and when my turn came going into the sitting-room, there were none of the usual amenities of the dentist's surgery, just a white enamel pail on the floor and an old-fashioned chair on which to sit. It was not an easy extraction – the tooth was an old one and was in bad condition – but for, I think, the only time in my life I experienced a perfect extraction without any feeling of pain from beginning to end. The dentist himself was delighted with his handiwork and I couldn't help being amused by the way he praised his own work. How he said, 'well, that was an excellent extraction. I am so glad that it has gone so well.' It is this kind of pride that Paul had, the pride of a surgeon when he has ended a difficult operation and the patient has come through, and healing has resulted. It is the kind of pride that every pastor ought to be able to have in his church, in his people. It is the kind of pride that Jesus Christ ought to have in those who have been redeemed and regenerate.

I wonder how far Christ is proud of us! I wonder how far he could say, concerning you and concerning me, as He watches us at our daily work, as He watches us in our family life, as He watches us walking down the street, I wonder if He ever points us out as it were to others and says, 'isn't that a wonderful Christian? I am so proud of him, I am so proud of her.' That was the final condition and conviction as far as Paul was concerned about the Church at Corinth – it was a Church that he was proud of. And it is from this that we draw the title for our study, the last study in this first section of this second epistle of Paul to the Church at Corinth, 'ALL'S WELL THAT ENDS WELL'.

QUESTIONS FOR DISCUSSION

Study No. 9 – II Corinthians 7:4–16

1. In this section we find Paul recording his pain, pleasure and finally his pride in the Corinthian Church.

   What would seem to be the real reasons for these emotions in the Christian pastor? Why should he reveal them?
2. 'What gives the pastor the right to criticise me? I'm a Christian!'

   For the speaker, this would be righteous indignation. But according to Paul, why has the pastor the right, indeed a duty, to criticise his people, and what should be their reaction as Christians?

Chapter 10

CHRISTIAN GIVING

Passage studied II Corinthians 8 and 9

It is interesting to note that Paul devotes two whole chapters to the matter of Christian Giving and also to note that it is the first thing to which he refers after reaching the conclusion that all was well again between himself and the Church at Corinth. This is what he stated at the end of chapter 7 'I rejoice therefore that I have confidence in you in all things'. I wonder if this is an unconscious but significant indication that Paul regards Christian giving as closely associated with spiritual health; that our giving is a kind of spiritual thermometer by which the condition of our health can be gauged; that there is an association between the spiritual state of a church and its financial state. Recently we have been suffering from the 'flu epidemic in our city and in every home clinical thermometers have been popped into people's mouths to test their health. I wonder if we were to take this thermometer and pop it into the mouths of churches what kind of a result we would get.

I have called our study this time 'Christian Giving' and it seems to me that there are three things that are meant to mark Christian giving as Paul sees it.

A. IT IS TO BE JOYFUL GIVING

The note of joy and thanksgiving is found again and again in these verses. Chapter 8:2 when speaking of the giving of the Macedonian Christians Paul speaks of 'the abundance of their joy'. Later on in chapter 9:7 he writes 'God loveth a cheerful giver' and the word in the Greek that is translated cheerful is the word from which we get our word hilarious. God loves a hilarious giver. All this confirms the words of our Lord recorded in Acts 20:35, though not recorded in the gospels, 'it is more blessed to give than to receive'. The translation of the word in English as blessed is a little bit unfortunate: it has a pious sound about it – almost unctuous: it means happy. This is how it is translated in the N.E.B. 'happiness lies more in giving than in receiving'. How true this is. The happy people in this world, the happy people in the life of the Church, are the givers, the givers of their money, of their time, of their strength, of their prayers. 'God loves a hilarious giver.' The kind of person who says 'hallelujah, here's the collection'. I have heard many 'hallelujahs' and many 'praise the Lords' spoken by Christians in meetings but I have never heard the announcement of the offering being received with a chorus of 'hallelujahs, praise the Lord, Amen'. But when you and I probe behind Christian giving as being a joyful giving we realise how true this is when we face two facts. The first is:

(a) *The motive of Christian giving*. And the motive is of course Christian love. Love is always concerned with others and never with itself, and this is what characterised supremely the two examples that Paul sets before the Corinthian Church. He quotes first of all the example of the Macedonians in chapter 8:2 following, and noting particularly the words in v.4 'Praying us with much intreaty' or as the R.S.V. puts it 'begging us earnestly for the favour of taking part in the relief of the saints'. Here was a Church that was itself passing through a time of deep poverty and persecution, and yet which motivated by a genuine Christian love was more concerned about the sufferings of others than about its own sufferings. The Church with which it was concerned was the Mother Church at Jerusalem. The other example quoted by Paul was the example of the Master, chapter 8:9 'You know the grace of our Lord Jesus Christ, that, though he was rich yet for your sakes he became poor, that ye through his poverty might be rich' 'for your sake' 'that ye might be rich'. The enrichment of others – this was the motive behind the Incarnation, and it is the Incarnation to which Paul is referring here. The Lord who left all the wealth and splendour and glory of heaven itself and stooped to the humility, to the poverty, of his earthly life in order that through that incarnation, involving of course the crucifixion and the resurrection, he might bring the wealth of God's pardoning and renewing grace into the lives of multitudes. The enrichment of others. This is the motivation of love. And in writing to the Church at Corinth Paul makes it clear, in chapter 8:8, that in speaking about giving his concern is that their love might be proved to be genuine. If there is no giving there is no loving, and now that he is assured of their loving he wants to see the proof of this in their giving. Love always longs to give. Love is never so happy as when, through its giving, it sees the happiness of others. I have quoted frequently some lines the source of which I have never been able to trace – these are the lines 'Love ever gives, forgives, outlives, and ever stands with open hands and while it lives it gives, for this is love's prerogative – to give, and give, and give'. The motive of Christian love makes Christian giving joyful. The other thing Paul speaks about is:

(b) *The measure of their giving*. Of the giving of the Macedonians he speaks in tones of amazement. J. B. Phillips translates, chapter 8:2 'Somehow, in most difficult circumstances, their joy and the fact of being down to their last penny themselves, produced a magnificent concern for others'. The N.E.B. translates 'they have shown themselves lavishly openhanded going to the limit of their resources and even beyond the limit, their giving surpassed our expectations for they gave their very selves to the Lord, and also under God to us'. Of the giving of the Master he says 'though he was rich, yet he became poor'. And so in the measure of Christian giving two things stand out: first the enrichment of those loved, and then impoverishment for those loving; and it is always so. There is an extravagance in love's giving without which love would not be content. Love never asks how little, but always how much. So again Paul warns later on that 'he which soweth sparingly shall reap sparingly, but he that soweth bountifully shall reap bountifully' and that we are to give 'not grudgingly'. And yet even while thinking in these terms Paul has his feet firmly on the ground. In chapter 8:13 he states 'Of course, I don't mean that others should be relieved to an extent that leaves you in distress'. My father always used to say 'be just before you are generous' and it is a dictum that would have found favour with Paul. Even our Lord warned against a kind of giving to God that ignored obligations and responsibility to one's own family. But allowing for these words of caution there is nevertheless a glad extravagance about love's giving; love gives lavishly and without regret to the needs of others and to the needs of God's work. So Christian giving is first of all joyful giving. The second thing about Christian giving that I find here in the mind of Paul is:

B. IT WAS CAREFUL GIVING

Lavishness did not mean carelessness. And I find two characteristics emerging in Paul's attitude to the whole question of the giving that he has in mind. He speaks first of all:

(a) *How sensibly the decisions must be reached.* Paul has spoken of lavish generosity but he qualifies this so sensibly by pointing out that God does not expect us to give what we do not have. God does not expect us all to give the same amount. Note chapter 8:12 'if there be first a willing mind, it is accepted according to that a man hath, and not according to that he hath not'. So common sense has not got to fly out of the windows. We are not to give (and this is the setting of the words we have already referred to) to such an extent that we enrich others to a degree which leaves us struggling in poverty, v.13. And this applies not simply to money but to time or strength. I know of many homes where Christian husbands give so much of their time to what they call the Lord's service that they have no time left for their wives and their families, and so while it may be they are enriching others they are impoverishing their own homes. What Paul has in mind here is that God evaluates our giving not by the amount so much as by the desire, and where there is love there is always an aching desire to give and this is what God is looking for and looking at. So in the decisions we make about our giving we are to act sensibly. God does not expect the impossible; God is not unfair or unjust in what he expects of us. This is where the conception of the tithe is so fair and so sensible. Many Christians feel that the ancient Jewish custom of giving a tenth of their income to God is one that a Christian should at least match if not exceed. The principle of the tithe means proportionate giving. If we give a tenth of what we have then those who have more will give more and those who have less will give less. This is what I mean by giving sensibly. The one thing of course we must not be content with is mere talk, or mere desire. The Corinthians had twelve months before taken the first steps to become involved in the work of relieving the poverty of the Church in Jerusalem. Paul wanted to see all that implemented by deeds – chapter 8:10. Indeed he reminds them in chapter 9:2 how originally their keenness in the past had been used by him as an inspiration to others. Now that the clouds of misunderstanding had cleared the words spoken months ago, the intentions expressed before the clouds of misunderstanding had arisen, these must be turned into deeds. How sensibly then the decisions must be reached, and:

(b) *How scrupulously the distribution must be made.* Christians are meant to be businesslike in their financial affairs, and here there must be complete integrity. And so from chapter 8:16 to chapter 9:5 Paul speaks of the measures he has taken to ensure this. He is sending three others to share in the whole matter – Titus, referred to in v.16 and then two who are not named. In v.18, one who is described as 'a brother whose praise is in the gospel throughout all the churches'. In v.22 another brother 'whom we have often tested' or proved. Here were two men, and it is quite suggestive and significant that they were not named. How much the Church owes to that great band of unknown workers whose praises, it may be, are unsung but who stand by and with others whose names may be well known are content to serve. And what a wonderful testimony each of these two men had. The one is described as a man whose praise was in all the churches; the other was described by Paul as a man who had been proved by him. This is tremendously challenging is it not? Some of us want to be workers in the fellowship of the Church. I wonder if we would have been chosen by Paul on either of these grounds. Is the quality of our life and testimony recognised by other Christians? Have the leaders in the Church proved and tested us and found us completely reliable and dependable? If we do not measure up to either of these conditions maybe it is our own fault that we are not used. Surely it is true to say that before God uses a man God proves a man; and this is the principle made out so clearly again and again in scripture that God always begins by giving us smaller jobs to do and when we have been found faithful in that which is least we can there prove our faithfulness in that which is great. The way to promotion in spiritual service is faithfulness and nothing can take the place of that. If we are unfaithful we will remain unused. But note the reason for Paul including these other men in the whole business of collecting and distributing the money. In vv.20 and 21 we read 'We intend that no one should blame us about this liberal gift which we are administering, for we aim at what is honorable not only in the Lord's sight but also in the sight of men'. 'But also in the sight of men' Paul realised how quickly people find fault. He wishes to guard against this on the financial aspect of his work by including others to see that everything was done decently and in order. Another reason of course for sending the men was to prepare the way for his own coming to Corinth. Paul had said so much to the Macedonian Church about the intentions of the Corinthians to share, and have fellowship, with the Church in Jerusalem and he didn't want to be let down and he didn't want the Corinthian Church to be let down, if and when he did come, bringing Macedonian Christians with him he found that the Corinthians had done nothing about their intentions after all. So Christian giving is meant to be joyful giving and careful giving. There is one other aspect about Christian giving that Paul finally deals with. Christian giving is to be:

C. FRUITFUL GIVING

Chapter 9:6 Paul is writing in terms of a sowing and a harvest. Christian giving is the kind of investment that any farmer makes when he sows his seed. It is an investment by love of money, time and strength. It is an investment that will bring results. It is a sowing that will be productive of a harvest. Paul has two things to say about this. The first is quite surprising: he speaks of:

(a) *The supply that will be assured.* If you are a giver God will see to it that you always have something to give. Chapter 9:8 'God is able to make all grace abound toward you; that ye, always having all sufficiency in all things, may abound to every good work'. The primary reference here is to things material rather than things spiritual, although the text could be widened out to include the latter. This is a wonderful thought is it not that if you are a giver God will see to it that you always have something to give. This is a very real and strong argument against those who sometimes say that a church cannot afford to give so much to Foreign Missions, that the need at home is so great. But the strange thing is that churches that do give generously to the work of God in other lands and in other ways these churches always seem to have the wherewithal to meet their own needs and to give what they desire to give. So the supply will be assured, and then Paul speaks of:

(b) *The sequel that will be achieved* A spirit of praise and thanksgiving will be created with all the ramifications that go with this. God will be praised. He is a giver, and when people sense the truth of this through the giving of His Church they will praise Him for what they now know Him to be. It is not just the meeting of a material need that is the result of Christian giving but the changing of the whole tone and attitude of the lives that receive. I am sure we can all think of lives that have been embittered because of the failure of the Christian Church to give to that life what it felt it had a right to receive. It may be of time, of sympathy, of understanding, even of material help. Such a life can become bitter and sour, and then later on another Christian comes and their attitude is quite different, they express the warmth and the concern and the love of God, and the heart that has been cold because of an earlier experience of the Church's failure warms to the love that is now being shown to it, and in that warming of the heart God will be praised. But not only will God be praised but they themselves would be blessed. v.13 suggests that their generosity will provide the evidence needed to convince others of the genuineness of their profession. The Christian Church in Jerusalem had grounds for being uncertain about the validity of Paul's work. He was moving amongst the Gentiles. But when they received the gifts that were the expression of Christian love and fellowship from the Gentile churches, this giving would result in a widening and deepening of the bonds of Christian fellowship and widening and extending of the fellowship of mutual prayer. The Church that received from them would in return pray for them, and what greater blessing can any Church have than to be prayed for, what greater blessing can any Christian have than to know that he is being prayed for. If a Church, if a Christian, gives to others then that Church and that Christian will receive so much in return – not necessarily financially or materially, but spiritually. All this reflects the truth of the words of our Lord 'Give, and it shall be given you; good measure, pressed down and shaken together and running over shall men give into your bosom. For with the same measure that ye mete withal it shall be given to you again.'

Christian Giving then is *Joyful Giving*, *Careful Giving*, and *Fruitful Giving*.

QUESTIONS FOR DISCUSSION

Study No. 10 – II Corinthians 8 and 9

1. How do the characteristics of the giving of the Macedonian Church compare with our own? Might people give more generously, if they consciously thought of 'taking part in the relief of saints'?
2. According to Paul, how should we regulate the giving of our money, time and energy? Discuss.
3. 'I don't understand why Christians give away so much of their money, instead of saving more for a rainy day, or investing their savings sensibly.'

   How sound are our investments with God? Consider the different ways in which the profits accrue.

Chapter 11

THE HARD CORE OF RESISTANCE

Passage studied II Corinthians 10:1–18

There are some scholars who feel that the contents of the following chapters are so different that they seem to be going back to a situation which existed prior to the conclusion reached in chapter 7:16 'I rejoice, because I have perfect confidence in you'. These scholars maintain that these chapters are part of the missing letter to which already reference has been made, and that through some mischance the pages of this missing letter have been inserted here and united with the second epistle. Professor Barclay accepts this position but Professor Denney rejects it. The position of Professor Denney seems perfectly logical. Confidence had indeed been restored with *almost* all the Christians at Corinth, but not with all. Following this restoration of confidence, Paul's pet concern for the Church at Jerusalem had immediately been shared with them, but now finally Paul turns to deal with the troublemakers – maybe very few in number, maybe with a sprinkling of sympathisers – and is dealing now specifically with them. To quote Denney 'It is as if all this had been dammed up in his heart for a long time'. There had been the taunts and the sneers that they had been casting up against the ministry of Paul and Paul now feels that it is time for them to be dealt with specifically. And so here we are dealing with this kind of situation which can exist in a Church, in a fellowship, where a small group have been causing trouble. As we probe beneath the language of this chapter, language which is not particularly easy to understand in the Authorised

Version (the New English Bible translation makes it much clearer and the Revised Standard Version also), there are quite obviously three areas of thought that are in the mind of Paul. First of all:

A. THE AUTHORITY OF THE PASTOR HAD BEEN DISCREDITED

Had he been too gentle in the way he had handled the situation? In the way he had handled these people? And had they mistaken his gentleness for weakness? Indeed had his gentleness encouraged them to go to yet further extremes of disloyalty in discrediting his ministry? As we read this section through Paul has three things to say along this line. First of all he speaks of:

(a) *The example of the Saviour.* Christ was one in whose ministry the note of authority had been sensed by all, although not obeyed by all, and yet Christ Himself had said of Himself, 'I am meek and lowly of heart'. And so Paul here introduces this section by referring to 'the meekness and gentleness of Christ'. Meekness, is the capacity to accept injury without resentment and praise without pride, and to learn from both. Gentleness, is a word used to describe the clemency of the judge who is good as well as just, and who recognises that adherence to the strict letter of the law may result in the perpetration of moral wrong. It is the gentleness which is prepared to exercise restraint for the sake of the ultimate and eternal spiritual good of those against whom outraged justice and anger might be tempted to act speedily but injuriously. How often this kind of situation does arise when the person injured would be acting within his rights, he might win his argument and his case but he would lose his man. Someone has said and it is worth repeating that there are two ways of opening a stiff lock: the one is to break it and the other is to oil it. Here Paul obviously has been trying to win over even this hard core of resisters with the oil of love. The second thing Paul takes note of here are:

(b) *The essentials for true success.* 'The weapons of our

warfare are not carnal, but mighty through God to the pulling down of strong holds.' The principles that govern spiritual effectiveness are totally different from those which govern natural inclinations and behaviour patterns. Because I don't lose my temper, because I don't come and lord it over the Church, because I don't get angry with you, because I don't order your expulsion, because I believe so differently from what you would have expected, don't think that my ways lack power and that they lack results. The weapons we use to achieve spiritual results are quite different from those that would be expected on the human level. They are not the weapons of human warfare but they have divine power. The weapons we use, the power we exercise is channelled so differently. Paul is thinking of the power of prayer, the power of Christian love, the power of the Holy Spirit. How the Church needs to grasp these lessons and put them into practice today. The example of His Saviour; the essentials of his success; and:

(c) *The elimination of himself.* 'Bringing every thought into captivity to the obedience of Christ.' This may be how Paul describes the ultimate goal he seeks to achieve in the lives of others, but he does so because it is the goal that he seeks to achieve in his own life. The secret of exercising authority is accepting authority and that authority the authority of Jesus Christ. This is the only authority that matters. Paul is not seeking to get others to do what he wants but he is seeking to get people to do what Christ wants: and that authority of Christ can only be discerned in a life in which that authority is displayed. And so Paul is not concerned in his conflict with the Corinthians to assert his own position, to have his own way: what he is concerned about is that both he and they may live lives of obedience to their one common Lord and Saviour, Jesus Christ.

The authority of the pastor had been discredited. Then also we see in this section:

B. THE APPEARANCE OF THE PASTOR HAD BEEN DERIDED

If the first taunt lay along the line that he had been too gentle with his critics, the second taunt was that he was too feeble in his whole appearance and personality. In v.10 Paul quotes his detractors as saying that 'his bodily presence is weak, and his speech contemptible' J. B. Phillips translates it 'his actual presence is feeble and his speaking beneath contempt'. Or putting it rather more bluntly as we might put it today, Paul as a minister was nothing to look at and no preacher at all. It is never a gracious or generous thing to descend to the level of insult in an argument. But Paul handles the harshness and unkindness of the insults of his enemies in his own way. He does not reply directly to what they have said but takes everything involved in their argument and their derision to a deeper level. He speaks of:

(a) *The reason for his ministry*. In v.8 he speaks of 'an authority which the Lord has given' in v.13 of 'the rule (or sphere) which God had apportioned to him'. The only reason he was doing what he was doing was because the Lord had called him – had called him to be an apostle. I know he says in v.7 that among you there are those that claim to be Christ's in a special way; but if they make that claim Paul has just as much right to make it too, and he does make it and asks that it should not be denied to him. To be in the place of the will of God, to be doing the work that God wants him to do, this is the only thing that can really satisfy the conscience of Paul or of any Christian. And the very fact that God had chosen him, the very fact that God had sent him, gave a dignity and an authority to his person and his task and his ministry that resided not in Paul but in the fact that he had been so called. This is one of the exciting things about being a Christian, to know that I am in the place that God wants me to be, to know that I am doing the work that God wants me to do, this is the only thing that really matters in life. It gives a meaning and a purpose that nothing else can. But Paul also directs the minds and eyes of his critics to:

(b) *The results of his ministry.* In v.7 R.S.V. reads 'Look at what is before your eyes'. The very existence of the Church was the result of Paul's obedience and Paul's ministry. Deride me, he says, scorn me if you like but don't shut your eyes to the facts before your face; don't close your minds to the blessing that God has given to my ministry, to the lives that God has changed through my ministry. He reminds them in v.14 'we were the first to come all the way to you with the gospel of Christ'. You may be right in all you say about my appearance, about my personality, but God has strange ways of working. So often He uses the weak things to destroy the mighty, the foolish people to humble the clever, to use the things that are not to bring to naught the things that are. After all what does it matter what a man looks like if he is efficient and capable at his job. We don't ask that our doctor be handsome, we ask that he be skilful: we don't ask that a person necessarily be smartly dressed, we ask that he be efficient at his job. These people may scorn and deride Paul's outward appearance – nothing to look at, no preacher at all, but that didn't alter the fact that he had done a wonderful work and that God had set His seal upon Paul's ministry. The reasons for his ministry; the results of his ministry; and:

(c) *The restraints on his ministry.* The only thing that was holding him back from venturing further to record yet greater exploits was the situation at Corinth. He refers to this in v.16 where he indicates that when things are better at Corinth there will be more attempted and more will be achieved. How often it is that time is wasted, energy is spent, progress is halted, dealing with unnecessary problems within the Church created by unthinking and difficult Christians, while all the time the task outside lies undone, the people outside remain unreached. No, Paul agrees, I may be nothing much to look at but God has called me, God has used me, and God has still more work for me to do if only you would let me get on with it. I am reminded of a great golfer in the top world class of golf. He carried a magnificent set of clubs around with him, all of them were beautiful clubs except one and that was his putter. His putter was out of the ark. It was an old, old club dating back into the days before clubs were made of stainless and rustless steel, but the thing that was important about this putter was not what it looked like but what the golfer could do with it and how he could putt. It was a little putter that his enemies dreaded the sight of. Paul was like that putter – nothing much to look at maybe, maybe nothing much of a preacher, but oh, how God could use the man, and this is the only thing that really matters. How far God had used him, and this is what he pleads as he handles his critics.

The authority of the pastor had been discredited: the appearance of the pastor had been derided: and finally:

C. THE ACHIEVEMENTS OF THE PASTOR HAD BEEN DISCOUNTED

He had been too gentle; he had been to feeble; he had been too humble. Even while Paul talks about the service he has sought to render to his Lord and to the Church he is aware of the difference in the whole approach between himself and his detractors. He knows that they despise him and so he replies by pointing out the way he thinks about his work, and there are three things here that Paul brings out. He speaks of:

(a) *The stupidity to which he will not stoop.* v.12 'they comparing themselves among themselves, are not wise'. Paul underlines the folly of getting our evaluation of our work from our friends, from those who like us, from those who think like us. He reminds them in v.18 it is not the person's own evaluation of his work that is valid. To do this is downright stupid and yet how prone we are – how prone they were. Just because we organised it then of course it must have been a success: just because it was our minister that had been asked to preach on an important occasion then it had to be a good sermon. This hard core of resisters to Paul no doubt had a great time applauding themselves. They had no ears for anything that anybody else had to say; they had no eyes for anyone else except their friends. Paul says this is a stupid way to think, to evaluate our own work and to evaluate the work of others. Paul just will not stoop to this kind of a level. And so he goes on to speak of:

(b) *A responsibility in which he will not fail.* Paul was alive to the fact that God had given him a work to do, God had given him a world to reach. For Paul it was not enough that there were Christians that he sought to serve but he was thankful that the Christians that he was serving were those whom he himself had led to Christ. How different was the attitude of the disturbers of the peace. They had come into a situation which had already been established by Paul. They had not led these Corinthians to Christ; but they were now leading them astray – indeed in the end they might even break away. Paul was troubled by this attitude, the attitude of people who could come in to another person's work and then blatantly appropriate it to themselves. There are still people like that, there are still sects like that. They make it a deliberate policy to go into a situation and then extract from it those who are prepared to listen to them. Professor Denney comments on this section of the chapter 'two feelings are compounded: the first an intense sympathy for the purpose of God that this gospel should be preached to every creature; and secondly, an intense scorn for the spirit that sneaks and poaches on another's ground'. And then Denney concludes by adding the significant comment 'The field is large enough for the efforts of all'. Neither Paul nor God has time for those who sheep steal in the work of Jesus Christ, and who glory in the fact that they have a fellowship around them and yet they themselves are not responsible for the spiritual life, the spiritual birth, the conversion of any of them. They have simply gone into other people's flocks and stolen some of their sheep. This is very far from the mind of Paul. Paul wants to do the work that God wants him to do, he doesn't want to enter in and build upon the work of another. And so finally, Paul speaks of:

(c) *A fidelity for which he can but pray*. In v.18 he speaks of 'the man whom the Lord commends'. It is told of Enoch, the man who walked with God, that he had this testimony 'he pleased God', and that was all that Paul wanted. The man whom the Lord commends. What a fantastic sentence this is to take, and then to measure ourselves up against it. In the life and work of any congregation there are always those who are craving for position, who are longing for power, who are never happy unless they are prominent. Paul is quite, quite different. He is not concerned about these things, he is not concerned what men think of him, what he is concerned about is what the Lord thinks of him. And this is his great desire – to be a man 'whom the Lord commends'. I wonder how far it would be true of you, I wonder how far it would be true of me that in all our thinking, in all our praying, in all our serving, in the life and fellowship of the Church of Jesus Christ, I wonder how far it would be true of you that you are a man, that you are a woman, 'whom the Lord commends'. If you are, if I am, then there is nothing else that really matters.

QUESTIONS FOR DISCUSSION

Study No. 11 – II Corinthians 10:1–18

1. Who would appear to have suffered most from the hard core of resistance – Paul, the Corinthian Church, the outside world?

What should be a pastor's main concern in dealing with persistent troublemakers?

2. What would be the effect on the life of the Church if every Christian really tried to 'compel every human thought to surrender in obedience to Christ'?
3. Consider the various weapons that the Christian can use to bring down 'every deceptive fantasy and every imposing defense that men erect against the true knowledge of God'.
4. What do we learn from Paul of the pastor's attitude and answer to the scorn and abuse that may be levelled at him?

Chapter 12

PAUL ANSWERS HIS DETRACTORS
or
PAUL TAKES OFF THE GLOVES

Passage studied II Corinthians 11:1–33

I would like to remind you that in this final section of Paul's letter to the Corinthians it would seem as if Paul is aiming his words at the small remnant of those who had been the cause of the trouble in the Corinthian Church: led by a small group of people who made great claims for themselves, a little cluster still remained of those who resented Paul's influence and who were critical of his ministry. In this chapter Paul is speaking in a way distasteful to himself but in a way that he feels is necessary to make his point. It would seem as if this is the only kind of language the people would understand to whom his words are directed. When we examine the chapter we find that there are three things that seem to emerge. First of all:

A. PAUL EXPLAINS HIS REASONS

Two things had motivated his conduct and his concern for the church in Corinth. First of all:
(a) *There must be no blemish in the Church.* v.2 'I feel a divine jealousy for you, for I betrothed you to Christ to present you as a pure bride to her one husband'. Jealousy has both a good and a bad aspect. For instance, God is described as 'a jealous God' – that is to say, deeply concerned for the wellbeing of those He loves. What Paul is getting at is that he doesn't want anything to mar the relationship that he had established between Christ and

the church at Corinth. There is in his heart a fastidious concern that will not tolerate the kind of interference that would spoil their conception of Christ and their relationship to Him. There is always something very wonderful about a new born faith and a newly kindled love for Christ, and Paul just could not stand by and watch others coming in and spoiling it all. The hymn writer put it this way 'Where is the blessedness I knew when *first* I saw the Lord?' There is a choice and a lovely blessedness about the first love in the life of an individual, or a new church, for the Lord. Christ, writing to one of the churches in the book of the Revelation makes this charge against them 'I have somewhat against thee because thou hast left thy first love'. But so many things can come in, so many ideas can spoil, and so we find Paul writing in v.3. 'I am afraid lest your thoughts will be led astray from a sincere and pure devotion to Christ.' This is what was the result of the activity of Paul's detractors. They were the agents but behind the agents Paul sensed the activity of the very Devil himself. His detractors had been presenting in v.4. 'Another Jesus,' they had been creating 'another spirit' they had been preaching 'another gospel'. These super apostles as Paul calls them, in all probability because this was the impression they liked to create, had obviously made a great impression at Corinth. They had had a good reception from this bunch who were obviously lacking in spiritual discernment. Their approach, their appearance, was seemingly more impressive than Paul's and Paul did not compare too well with them. This kind of situation can still exist within the life of the visible church. Some people are so lacking in spiritual discernment they can say of a minister 'he is such a nice man'. The fact that he doesn't preach Christ, that he doesn't preach God's Word seems immaterial to them. We should be concerned about the Christ this man presents, about the kind of church he builds. So many churches are little more than social clubs and in so many churches there is very little going on that could not go on equally well in a synagogue. But they say, 'he is such a nice man'. A nice man indeed says Paul, why he is a minister of the Devil. This is the first concern in the mind of Paul, there must be no blemish in the Church, and the second:

(b) *There must be no burden on the Church* vv.7–12. It is made abundantly plain in scripture that those who are the pastors over the Church are to be kept materially by the Church, but when it comes to evangelism the picture is quite different. It would seem as if Paul never asked for money when he came to establish a Church through the preaching of the gospel but once the Church was firmly established he never hesitated to ask them to accept this responsibility. This is why I personally feel it is never right to have a collection in a Church or in an evangelistic crusade. It isn't right that we should ask people to pay for the privilege of being converted. The gospel is free. Christians accept this responsibility always, but we should not ask the unconverted to accept it. Another thing that may have influenced Paul is that in his time teachers were highly esteemed. It was expected of them that their expenses would have to be met. This had led to a kind of false evaluation of a man's worth. The bigger the fee the bigger the man. The trouble was that Paul had done nothing of this, He had worked with his hands. He had received indeed timely support from other churches in Macedonia, most likely from Philippi. But then these other teachers had acted so differently. They had been demanding in material things and domineering in every other way, and just because they had acted like this some people without spiritual discernment had thought they must therefore be bigger and better men. And so Paul writes in v.20 'You seem to like it if a man makes slaves of you, or preys upon you, or takes advantage of you, or puts on airs and insults you'. There had been those in Corinth so lacking in discernment that they had been deceived into thinking that these men were the real thing and Paul in comparison was a nonentity. Paul admits in v.6 that he has no gifts of oratory but he goes on to say he at least knows what he is talking about and what the gospel is. His motives were those of love. He didn't want to give any grounds at all for any argument or any criticism being made of him that would bring dishonour upon the name of Christ. This is why he had made no charge upon the material resources of those to whom he had come to preach the gospel. And so Paul explains his reasons behind his attitude and actions – there was to be no blemish in the Church and no burden on the Church. And then Paul really takes the gloves off, and the second strand we find in this chapter centres round:

B. PAUL EXPOSES HIS RIVALS

We live in an age when toleration is exalted to a place it doesn't deserve and certainly doesn't have in the mind of God. We have almost reached the stage of tolerating anything and everything. God's Word draws a very different picture. In Hebrews 1:9 we read 'Thou hast loved righteousness, and hated iniquity'. There is an intolerance in the very character of God. He loves the sinner but He hates the sin. Someone has put it this way 'It is possible to value toleration so much that clear cut distinctions between right and wrong may become impossible' and I think we might add – between truth and error. And so when Paul finds that forces and people are at work to destroy the Church of Jesus Christ he is fearless and he is merciless in what he says. And we need to remember that this is exactly what our Lord did: when He had something to say about the Scribes and Pharises, he was blunt. Paul has two things to say about these workers in Corinth. First of all:

(a) *They were deceptive.* v.13 'disguising themselves as the apostles of Christ'. Paul speaks of the tactics of Satan as being the tactics they follow. It is not quite clear what the reference is in v.14 when Paul speaks of Satan himself as being 'transformed into an angel of light' but what Paul is getting at is absolutely plain – mainly the fact that discernment is always needed; that when Satan would tempt us or divert us from the will of God he does not do this by presenting us with something obviously evil or obviously erroneous but with something that seems to be very like God's will or God's truth, something reasonable, something acceptable. It really is a frightening thought that within the sphere of the religious life of the Church there are those who are in Paul's words 'the ministers of Satan'. There may be a fine building, there may be beautiful music but the truth as it is in Christ is absent. Christ of course may be recognised and indeed reverenced, but not as the Son of God or Saviour of men. And the people there are 'such nice people' but all the time they are 'ministers of Satan'. Ministers of the Church and yet at the same time ministers of the Devil presenting a Christ who is no Christ. We are familiar with counterfeits in life. Anything of value has its counterfeit. I remember so well at Rome airport many years ago being offered what looked like a Parker pen. We were told that they had been sold by Americans in exchange for cigarettes – actually they had been made in Japan, and when we examined them very closely we found that the word Parker on the pen was spelt P.arker so they were P.arker pens but so like the real thing that anybody could be deceived unless they were particularly observant. We need to have our minds on the alert. Deceptive, and:

(b) *They were destructive.* v.20. This is how Paul describes the result of their preaching and their practices 'they make slaves of you, they prey upon you, they take advantage of you, they put on airs and strike you on the face'. The enslavement of which Paul speaks may have been enslavement to a whole system of Jewish rules and regulations which Paul had seen had been abolished in Christ. It may have been enslavement to themselves but their followers were not allowed to do or think except what they permitted them to do or think. This enslavement was accompanied by material impoverishment. Where Paul took nothing, they took plenty. And in doing all this they were insultingly arrogant. I want to say that all this is not ancient history: it is happening today, and the incredible thing is that there are plenty of people who are prepared to take it all. How different was the gospel that Paul had preached. The pure light of the truth as it is in Christ and the perfect liberty that men found in Him – this was what Paul had preached. This was what the Corinthians had believed, and now Paul saw all this imperilled. No wonder Paul takes the gloves off: no wonder he exposes his rivals. Deceptive and destructive. These are strong words but they are spoken by a strong man. There is a time and there is a place for this kind of language still. Paul explains his reasons: Paul exposes his rivals: and:

C. PAUL EXAMINES HIS RECORD

And this he does from v.17 to the end of the chapter. What Paul is saying is 'this kind of talk is crazy but as it seems to be the kind of language you understand, the kind of language these super apostles use, well I'll have a go at a bit of boasting too, though I am going to tell you right away this is not the way the Lord would have me or any other servant of His talk'. Two things about Paul's record are worth noting. First of all:

(a) *The wonder of his record.* Paul begins by stating his authentic Jewish background, and the fact that he begins with this suggests that these 'super apostles' were Judaisers. They were people who wanted to burden the Christian Church with all the ritual and rigmarole of Jewish religion and habit, and so Paul takes them up on this ground and he speaks racially first of all. In v.22 he says, 'Are they Hebrews? So am I. Are they Israelites? So am I. Are they the seed of Abraham? So am I.' Paul never forgot he was a Jew, although he was supremely and first of all a Christian. This throws an interesting light upon the fact that very often our past can play an important part in our present usefulness in the service of God. The fact that Paul was a Jew gave him a lever here that helped him to present his case. But having dealt with the matter racially he then goes on to speak of the matter spiritually. 'Are they ministers of Christ' he asks. 'I am more' or as the R.S.V. translates it 'I am a better one'. And then follows the most incredible list of sufferings. As we read this list through it helps us realise how little we really know of Paul. Most of what is mentioned here is not mentioned anywhere else. This suffering was on the material and physical level, and then Paul says, 'and you must add to that all the suffering that I have on the spiritual and mental plane' in v.28 what he calls 'the care of all the churches'. And so Paul stresses the fact that suffering is part of the authentic mark of the genuine servant, and one can almost feel that he wants to turn round and say to these, who are seeking to detract from his position and influence, 'Do you have a record like this?' 'Can you point to scars in your bodies as I can point to scars in mine?' Do you remember how writing to the Galatians chapter 6:17 Paul said 'henceforth let no man trouble me: for I bear in my body the marks of the Lord Jesus Christ'. It is not people who talk big that really matter in the service of Jesus Christ, it is those who are prepared to suffer. And so Paul ends on an extremely high note. Having spoken of the wonder of his record, he ends by speaking about:

(b) *The witness to his record.* v.31 'God . . . knoweth that I lie not'. What a staggering claim to make. Here was a man with nothing to hide and nothing to fear. Could the others claim as much? Paul's argument here is unanswerable. If suffering is the hallmark of Christian service then sincerity in the sight of God is the other. It was said of Charles Haddon Spurgeon, the great Baptist preacher, that on one occasion he is quoted as having said these words 'you could take the story of my life and write it across the skies, I have nothing to hide'. What an amazing claim to make. This was the claim that Paul was making, and he was turning on his enemies and saying to them 'Can you make the same claim?' Is your service marked with the same suffering and is it marked with the same complete and utter sincerity? Can God Himself bear witness to the quality of your service, so called?' Somebody put it delightfully in this way 'Paul wore his sufferings as a soldier wears his decorations'.

QUESTIONS FOR DISCUSSION

Study No. 12 – II Corinthians 11:1–33

1. What should be the prime concern of the pastor – the relationship of his people to himself or to Christ? What conclusions are we forced to draw – according to Paul – about those pastors who are concerned primarily with their own image? Do you agree?
2. Paul claims that his detractors are instruments of Satan, and that the ultimate effect of their activity will be that the Church at Corinth will 'lose its first love'.

   Consider Paul's view, and in the light of it the tendency that some people have of voicing criticism of a man whose ministry has been owned of God.
3. Why is it important that a pastor should include teaching in his ministry, and encourage discernment of the truth in young converts?
4. Amy Wilson Carmichael has a poem which concludes:

   'Can he have followed far
   Who has no wounds, no scar?'

   Consider some of the hall-marks of the genuine pastor.

Chapter 13

FROM DIFFICULTY, THROUGH DISCOVERY, INTO DOXOLOGY

Passage studied II Corinthians 12:1–10

We come in our study now to one of the most treasured passages amongst all the writings of St. Paul; treasured by Christians who have known something of difficulty in their lives and who desire to find God's answer to their problems in Christ. Among the earliest of the addresses I ever gave at Keswick there is one on this passage of scripture. I titled that message on which God's blessing graciously rested as 'The Discipline Of Disappointment'. Under that title the message has been published and widely distributed, and is also included in one of my books. One of the exciting things about the Bible is that one can come back to a passage and find new light where one thought one had seen all the light there was. And so it was that in later years when I was studying the passage again a new title came to my mind and a new message, a fuller message I believe. I titled it 'From Difficulty, Through Discovery, Into Doxology'. I have once again done my homework, I have read my translations of this particular passage, and read my commentaries to see if there might be some fresh light upon the passage, a fresh outline maybe that would sum up its content and meaning for us. We might have called it – THE CONFLICT OF THE SOUL: THE CONCERN OF THE SAVIOUR: AND THE COMING OF THE SONG: but I feel to do this would be to take away from the earlier outline that God gave me, and so I am going to go back to that familiar outline and maybe bring some fresh thoughts following the main structure of that message. In a sense what we will be doing tonight will be rather like being invited to go round a beautiful garden that we know well but in which we can always see something fresh, a garden whose beauty and fragrance is one that fills our hearts with praise and thanksgiving. This analogy is apt because the word paradise translated means a walled garden, and Paul apparently feels that the experience God gave him was rather like being shown round a beautiful garden full of fruit and flower and fragrance. So let us come to the message of these choice verses when Paul recalling an experience that happened to him some fourteen years previously shares its meaningfulness with the Christians at Corinth. I believe that this passage may enable us, in the words of Dr. Stuart Holden, to transform what he calls 'the thorn pain into the triumph song'. This is possibly the most intimate and most revealing passage in all the epistles. The great apostle draws aside the veil of natural reserve and shares with the Church at Corinth and with us one of those hours of spiritual crisis that stand like milestones along the pilgrim way.

A. THERE IS DIFFICULTY HERE

How easy it is for us to think that great Christians have no problems, that those who appear to us to be spiritual giants have an easy time. They seem to know all the answers, their lives seem to display an easy mastery, their words are words of authority and experience, their service for God bears a quality and an effectiveness that make our efforts seem poor and amateurish. And in the consciousness of the magnitude of the problems that we have to face and the feebleness of our efforts to solve them we look almost enviously at such lives and we say, 'it is all very well for him', 'it is all very well for her'.

I wonder how often people must have said that about Paul – 'it's easy for him'. This passage shows us how wrong such an attitude would have been for them, and how wrong such an attitude could be for us, for here in the heart of this the greatest of all Christians there lay a problem that seemed to defy all solution, a pressure that to him was almost unbearable. Let us look then with reverence and let us learn. As we consider Paul's difficulty we note first of all:

(a) *A pressure that seemed unhelpful.* He calls it 'a thorn in the flesh, the messenger of Satan to buffet me'. What precisely it was we do not know but from this description we can gather enough to let us see something of what it meant to Paul. Commentators differ as to whether this was a reference to something physical or something spiritual. Paul uses the words 'the flesh' in either sense and I personally am convinced that this is something spiritual. Paul is referring to the flesh in the sense of the old carnal nature within. It may have had physical involvements but basically Paul is dealing with something spiritual here. In its origin it seemed satanic – he calls it 'the messenger of Satan', in its object it seemed to be a major hindrance in his life and work. He calls it 'the messenger of Satan to buffet me'. R.S.V. and J. B. Phillips translate 'to harass me' the N.E.B. translates 'to bruise me'. The word is a strong one, it means to buffet with a fist. Here was something utterly frustrating, something which left Paul bruised and beaten. Paul was harassed by it, frustrated by it. I wonder if there are any harassed Christians here! In its outcome this thorn in the flesh seemed to make Paul conscious of the old nature within, to arouse it, to awaken it, to make Paul aware of it. It tended as we might say to bring out the worst in him. Do we know anything of this kind of situation? We have no doubt but the Devil is behind; we find it utterly frustrating; if only it wasn't there then everything would be wonderful, but it is there and every time we are confronted by it the old nature – the flesh – is aroused to activity within and brings out the worst in us, our temper, our pride, our lust, our self-will. A pressure that seemed unhelpful. The other aspect of this difficulty lay in:

(b) *A prayer that seemed unheard.* v.8 'For this thing I besought the Lord thrice that it might depart from me'. Paul did what all of us do about problems and pressures like this – he prayed about it, and behind that prayer was the conviction in the mind of Paul that this thing had to go. He did not simply pray but he prayed with the specific intention 'I besought the Lord thrice that it might depart from me'. This thing was a hindrance and in the mind of Paul it had to go. It was a hindrance in his life, it was a hindrance in his service – he would be far better without it. Paul was quite clear about that. Have you and I ever prayed that kind of prayer? We want something, someone, some situation, to be dealt with by God. It has simply got to end or our whole life as Christians will be spoiled, our testimony and usefulness will be ruined. But as Paul prayed it seemed as if his prayer was unheard – once he prayed, twice he prayed, three times he prayed, and one can imagine the intensity of desire that lay behind Paul's praying. Was there a tinge of complaint, almost of reproach? Why did he have to ask the Lord three times that it might be taken away? How often have you and I prayed about our problems, the pressures in our lives that have seemed unhelpful? Far more times maybe than that. Is there however a lesson that we need to learn? Paul started praying and then he stopped praying. I wonder if God interrupted him: I wonder if God wants to interrupt us. In v.9 we read 'and he said unto me' and the tense there is the perfect tense. It means, he did say and has been saying to me ever since. Has God got to remind some of us of a need to listen, instead of to go on asking? What would God say to you, what will He go on saying to me? If there is difficulty here then:

B. THERE IS DISCOVERY HERE

As Paul listened so he learned, when Paul stopped talking God started speaking, and God spoke of two things. First of all:

(a) *The unrecognised purpose of God* v.7 'lest I should be exalted above measure' or as J. B. Phillips translates it more dramatically 'to prevent my becoming absurdly conceited'. Twice Paul records these words. It would seem as if the lesson was well learned. There was one danger that dogged the steps of this greatly used man, this greatly blessed Christian. A danger that it would seem Paul never sensed but God sensed it, and God now shares it with His servant, and the danger was simply that of pride. With such a record behind him how easily Paul could have become proud, and had he become proud he would therefore have become useless. Spurgeon has a great sermon on the text 'supposing Him to be the gardener'. The gardener knows the soil that suits the plant, and sometimes he plants the soul in the soil of sorrow and of suffering. It was because God knew, that He planned things this way and permitted 'the messenger of Satan to buffet' His servant. This was permitted to achieve one purpose only but that a vital purpose. It was there to keep Paul a humble and therefore a usable Christian 'lest I should be exalted'. I don't know what may be the special area in your life or mine that God knows to be in need of special care. It may be there is something lacking in our character, something lacking that could therefore endanger our witness: it may be there is something that needs to be preserved. But always behind the pressure there is the purpose of a God of perfect love, perfect wisdom and perfect power. Many of you will remember the poem written by Amy Wilson Carmichael of Dohnavur. She recalls in this poem an experience that came to her when she was three years old, but so vivid was the experience that it left an indelible mark upon her mind and she recalled in these words:

Just a tiny little child, three years old
And a mother with a heart all of gold.
Often did that mother say,
'Jesus hears us when we pray
For He's never far away
And He always answers'.

Now that tiny little child had brown eyes
And she wanted blue instead, like blue skies:
For her mother's eyes were blue,
Like forget-me-nots. She knew
All her mother said was true,
Jesus always answered.

So she prayed for two blue eyes, said goodnight,
Went to sleep in deep content and delight.
Woke up early, climbed a chair
By a mirror. Where! Oh where
Could the blue eyes be? Not there!
Jesus hadn't answered.

Hadn't answered her at all. Never more
Could she pray. Her eyes were brown, as before.
Did a little soft wind blow?
Came a whisper, soft and low
Jesus answered. He said, 'no'.
Isn't 'No' an answer?

Little did that little girl of three years old with her brown eyes know that God's purpose for her lay in India. In India where she was to become the 'mother' of thousands of unwanted temple children, where she was to become an Indian. She needed those brown eyes and God knew it, although she didn't. Have you ever met an Indian woman with blue eyes? No, their eyes are always brown, and God had given her the eyes that she needed. The unrecognised

purpose of God: but there is something more here that Paul was to discover and that was:
(b) *The unrestricted plenitude of grace.* What did God say to him and keep on saying to him? 'My grace is sufficient for thee.' It is important to note that this is not a promise it is a statement 'My grace *is* sufficient for thee' therefore there is no need to escape from the pressure. Paul, you want this thing to go – not only would that be unwise but it would be quite unnecessary. There is no need to escape when God's grace is sufficient and there is therefore no room for excuse. So often we make the pressure of some persistent problem become an excuse for lowering our standards. We say, 'you would need the patience of Job to keep your temper'. You don't need the patience of Job when you have the patience of Jesus. 'My grace *is* sufficient.' This is a present tense statement. Grace is never experienced in anticipation but at the moment of need it is there, and it is sufficient. There is difficulty then: there is discovery: and finally there is:

C. THERE IS DOXOLOGY HERE

And here the thorn pain is transformed into the triumph song. If this experience is to be ours let us follow Paul here and note:
(a) *How Paul's attitude is changed.* 'Most gladly therefore will I rather' N.E.B. translates 'I shall therefore prefer'. What would Paul prefer? What would Paul rather have? Well surely he is simply saying that he'd rather that this pressure stayed. Would we dare to follow him here? We have seen how Paul prayed that this thing might be taken away from him, and now instead of praying for it to be taken away he is saying he'd rather that it remained. I don't know what the pressure is in your life that seems so desperate that you want to be rid of it – it's such a hindrance it simply must go; but could you dare you; could I, dare I, look at that thing and say to God, knowing that something is involved in it of infinite

worth and value, 'we'd rather it stayed'? Paul's attitude is changed and:

(b) *Paul's acceptance is complete.* He says, 'there was given to me' and of course the gift was from the Lord's hand ultimately. But a gift has to be accepted. It is not enough for us to submit to these circumstances but to accept them. And Paul accepts this gladly because he has found that the gift is a gateway to an experience of Christ's sufficiency that could never be his any other way. v.9 'Most gladly therefore will I rather glory in my infirmities that the power of Christ may rest upon me.' And here is his final testimony, v.10 'I take pleasure in infirmities, in reproaches, in necessities, in persecutions, in distresses for Christ's sake: for when I am weak, then am I strong.' Some time ago I came across a poem which puts this in words that to me are quite unforgettable. The poem is entitled:

'Accept It'

Accept it. From Thy hand, dear Lord, I take
This hurting thing and bear it for Thy sake.
Nor bear it only, but in Thy dear name,
Thy strength, Thy power, to love it Lord, I claim;
To love it till from struggles, toil and tears,
The likeness of Thy life in me appears.
Accept it. From Thy hand this thing I take,
Lord, make it glorious for Thine own name's sake.

QUESTIONS FOR DISCUSSION

Study No. 13 – II Corinthians 12:1–10

1. 'It's easy for him to be a radiant, victorious Christian.'
   When we consider Paul's experience, have we the right to say this of anyone? Consider the inner ministry of grace that may have led to the outward victory and radiance.
2. Some people say, 'If only I could be rid of this problem!'

while Paul elsewhere says, '*In all* these things we *are more than conquerors* through Him who loved us.'

Consider Paul's words carefully, in particular what they reveal of the sphere, the scale and the source of the victory of which he felt so certain.

3. Would you care to discuss any 'thorns in the flesh' that you are aware of in your own experience, and consider whether they are sent by Satan or by God, and how God can be glorified in them.

Chapter 14

PAUL'S FINAL APPEAL

Passage studied II Corinthians 12:11–13:14

We come to the end of our series of studies in Paul's letters to the Christian Church at Corinth under the title 'Pastor and People'. Professor Barclay introduces his comment on this section with the words 'this section reads like the words of a man who has put out some tremendous effort and who at the end of it is weary. It almost seems as if Paul is limp with the effort that he has made.' Denney in his commentary puts it this way, 'in this section we feel the ground-swell of the storm that has been raging'. I am sure that most of us must have seen the sea restlessly heaving when the violence of the storm has spent itself: The boats at anchor, rolling uneasily with a sound of creaking ropes and creaking masts. And so there is still an element of unease in this final section as Paul makes his final appeal to the hard core of those who had, as yet, still held out against his position and ministry. So here we have Paul's conclusion of the whole matter and his final appeal. Here are the main points contained in this section. We find:

A. THE FINAL REBUKE THAT PAUL GIVES

After excusing himself again for having spoken so much of himself, so foolishly and so boastingly, Paul administers his final words of rebuke to his opponents and he speaks of:

(a) *The debt they owe to his ministry.* v.11 'I ought to have been commended by you'. Those who were still hostile to Paul were either hostile on the grounds of their adherence to Jewish traditions or hostile on the grounds of their reluctance to part with pagan practices, and so they were against Paul for what he said and for what he was. But he reminds them that the Church at Corinth owed him a tremendous debt 'I ought to have been commended by you. I am not inferior to these super apostles. The signs of a true apostle were performed among you in all patience (or endurance).' The fact is, he says, that instead of running me down you ought to be praising me up. Look at what has happened through my ministry. Look at the change in your lives. Look at the Christ you have come to know. Look at the Church that has now come into existence. What a way to treat the one to whom under God you owe so much; The one on whose ministry God has so obviously set His seal. Ingratitude is the grounds of the rebuke that Paul gives to these men in a last desperate attempt to win them over and soften their hearts and their attitude. How tragically up to date the Bible is for this situation can still exist in a Church. There can still be some who overlook the fact that God has manifestly set His seal upon the ministry in their midst and instead of thanking God for what God has done they make it difficult, if not impossible, for God's servant to exercise the ministry to which he has been called by God. These people need to be reminded of the debt that a congregation can owe to the ministry under God of His servant. But Paul also goes on to speak of:

(b) *The doubt they cast on his ministry*. He writes in v.11b 'I am not at all inferior to these superlative apostles, even though I am nothing'. You have been discrediting me, he says. You have said that I am nothing much to look at; that I am no preacher at all to listen to. And of course criticism and the work of discrediting a person is easy. It can have a basis in truth but it need have no basis in truth, all it needs is that the slur and the slander be launched. The reason apparently in Corinth was that Paul was not showy enough or maybe that he was not accommodating enough, and most extraordinary of all that he was not expensive enough. These critics had a false standard of estimating the worth of a servant of God. They estimated his worth by the price or fee that he exacted. These other men who had come in as leaders were expensive. Paul, apparently by making no charge, had in effect not only devalued himself but had devalued the Church that he served. They feel as if he had almost insulted them, and so he apologizes for having done this wrong – v.13. He explains that the reason was, however, the selflessness of his love. He said, I didn't want your money I wanted your salvation. We find ample evidence in Paul's writings that he did not hesitate to lay an obligation on any Church to maintain the ministry in its midst, but in the work of evangelism or in his work in certain Churches that were maybe young and struggling, or maybe where certain circumstances existed that made him decline their financial help, Paul was prepared to do the work without expecting anything in return. He uses an illustration here from the family – v.14 – the parents provide for the young children; it is not expected that the young children will provide for the parents. The trouble was that the charge had been enlarged to suggest that even if Paul did not after all get some money from the Churches he had helped yet he did get some from those he had sent later as his agents. Paul ends this section in v.15 with an appeal that has a note of pathos within it. 'For all this,' he says, 'am I to be loved the less?' Ingratitude is never easy to bear, and when one has as St. Paul says been willing to spend himself and be spent, for people to turn round and criticise and condemn needs every ounce of God's grace. But having noted the final rebuke that Paul gives, we go on to note:

B. THE SPIRITUAL RESPONSE THAT PAUL SEEKS

Beginning at v.19 we have two threads of thought running through this next section. First of all Paul speaks of:

(a) *The motives that constrain him in his service.* And all his motives have to do with the spiritual good of those he is seeking to help. He is concerned supremely with their progress, their upbuilding v.19. And so we read again in chapter 13:7 'We pray God you may not do wrong, that you may do what is right'. Paul is disturbed and afraid lest when he comes he finds things otherwise than they should have been; that instead of being able to rejoice with the spiritual progress they have made he would be humbled and shamed in the sight of God by the condition in which he would find the Church, so tragically other than what it ought to have been. How many a minister has shared the feelings and emotions of St. Paul. A minister leaves a Church and is away for several years maybe and then he returns, in what condition is he going to find those to whom his ministry had been so richly blessed of God? Would he find that they have gone on and grown and matured, or would he find that they have gone back? Many people in St. George's-Tron owe a great debt to the ministry of Tom Allan but supposing Tom Allan was to return, supposing he was to come back and meet those who had received much blessing under his ministry, would he rejoice or would he be put to shame? This is the situation that is in the mind of Paul as he speaks of the possibilities that fill his heart with foreboding in vv.20 and 21. But if he is disturbed and afraid he is also determined – nothing will make him turn aside from his purpose and so he warns those who are hostile to his ministry that they will not be spared when he comes again. Chapter 13:2 'I warned those who sinned before and all the others, and I warn them now while I am absent, as I did when present on my second visit, that if I come again I will not spare them'. Paul is prepared to have a showdown if need be. As Professor Barclay says, 'if healing medicines fail there is nothing for it but the surgeon's knife'. These were the motives that constrain him in his service as he seeks a spiritual response from the Church, and he also speaks of:

(b) *The Master that controlled him in his service.* 'Don't think' he says in chapter 12:19 'that in all this boasting I have been trying to gain favour with you. I serve another Master. It is in the sight of God that we have been speaking to you in Christ.' What you think of us is a matter of indifference as long as you are making progress. 'I hope' he says, 'you will find that we have not failed, but my concern is not that we may appear to have met the test, but that you may do what is right.' Chapter 13:7. That you may progress even if, in your eyes, we have been a failure. And so he goes on to say in v.9. 'We are glad when we are weak and you are strong. What we pray for is your improvement.' And so in this section Paul gives a final rebuke and seeks a spiritual response, and then finally we see also here:

C. THE PRACTICAL REQUEST HE MAKES

And there are two things that Paul asks of the Christian Church at Corinth, and particularly of this section that remains hostile and critical. I want us to note them as we close. Let us note:

(a) *Where he asks them to look.* Chapter 13:5 'examine yourselves' Test yourselves. These folk have been looking at him. Paul says, it is time you looked at yourselves, and these words are in the present tense – keep examining yourself; keep testing yourselves; keep proving yourselves to see indeed if you are in the faith at all. Even the very fact of their being Christians at all is almost suspect in the light of the behaviour that they have been displaying. And if they are Christians what kind of Christians are they? Are they really Christians in whom Christ is dwelling? Is this the way that the indwelling Christ would have them live? Criticize me if you like, says Paul, that's O.K. but why don't you criticize yourselves? What kind of Christians are you, you who talk so big, you who say so much about my failures. What about your failures? What a sensible bit of advice this is. So often the people who say most in a Church are those who do least, and Paul's counsel is wise. He asks us to look just where he asked them to look – 'examine yourselves'. But if we see here where he asks them to look, we see also:

(b) *How he asks them to live* In v.11 'Live in peace, and the God of peace and love will be with you'. Cut out all this divisive thought and talk and God's blessing will be yours. It is possible for Christians to create an atmosphere in which God cannot work. Do you remember how James spoke of this in his epistle. The epistle of James chapter 3:18 'And the harvest of righteousness is sown in peace by those who make peace'. When we examine the words of James we realise that there is a soil in which spiritual work can prosper and there is also a soil in which spiritual work finds it difficult to grow. Paul realises that if this little group go on with their criticism, their fault finding, with their squabbling, with their whispering, with their talking, the work of the Church will suffer, and so he says, 'live in peace, and the God of love and peace will be with you'.

And so this great letter ends with some of the most familiar words, spoken more frequently possibly than any others in the Christian Church, the words of the Benediction 'The grace of the Lord Jesus Christ and the Love of God and the fellowship of the Holy Spirit be with you all. Amen.'

QUESTIONS FOR DISCUSSION

Study No. 14 – II Corinthians 12:11–13:14

1. What should be our first concern and responsibility – our own standing as Christians or the status of others?
2. What does the true pastor primarily aim at in teaching his flock, and what does he look for in his Christian people?
3. In what sort of fellowship can 'the grace of the Lord Jesus' best be seen?

4. We have been concerned primarily with the contest between Paul and his detractors.

   Consider the role of the mature Christian in a fellowship or church where there is bitter criticism of a ministry which is clearly owned of God.

These Bible studies were recorded when originally delivered in Glasgow. The tapes may be hired or bought by writing to the author c/o St. George's-Tron church, Buchanan Street, Glasgow, Scotland, U.K.